J. Coxon

FUNCTION POINT ANALYSIS

Prentice Hall Advanced Reference Series

Computer Science

FUNCTION POINT ANALYSIS

J. BRIAN DREGER

PRENTICE HALL

Englewood Cliffs, New Jersey 07632

Library of Congress Cataloging-in-Publication Data

Dreger, J. Brian.
   Function point analysis / J. Brian Dreger.
      p.   cm. — (Prentice Hall advanced reference series)
   Includes index.
   ISBN 0-13-332321-8
   1. Software productivity—Measurement. 2. Function point
     analysis. I. Title.
   QA76.76.P74D74 1989
005.3—dc19   88-39415
                                        CIP

Editorial/production supervision
   and interior design: *Gertrude Szyferblatt*
Manufacturing buyer: *Mary Ann Gloriande*

Prentice Hall Advanced Reference Series

The publisher offers discounts on this book when ordered
in bulk quantities. For more information, write:
      Special Sales/College Marketing
      College Technical and Reference Division
      Prentice Hall
      Englewood Cliffs, New Jersey 07632

Printed in the United States of America

10 9 8 7 6 5 4 3

ISBN 0-13-332321-8

PRENTICE-HALL INTERNATIONAL (UK) LIMITED, *London*
PRENTICE-HALL OF AUSTRALIA PTY. LIMITED, *Sydney*
PRENTICE-HALL CANADA INC., *Toronto*
PRENTICE-HALL HISPANOAMERICANA, S.A., *Mexico*
PRENTICE-HALL OF INDIA PRIVATE LIMITED, *New Delhi*
PRENTICE-HALL OF JAPAN, INC., *Tokyo*
SIMON & SCHUSTER ASIA PTE. LTD., *Singapore*
EDITORA PRENTICE-HALL DO BRASIL, LTDA., *Rio de Janeiro*

TO

Barbara,

Eddy, Susan, Barbara Jo, and Paul

CONTENTS

FIGURES

FOREWORD

"The function-point method is the most effective metric yet developed for information systems. It is now possible to use the function-point total to predict source-code size (as well as business value, cost, and project duration, all with exceptional accuracy—JBD) in any of 250 or more languages. The technique is rapidly spreading throughout the world."

In 1988, the computer era is approximately 45 years old and has spawned one of the greatest industries in human history. The use of computers is now so pervasive that all major corporations and most minor ones are absolutely dependent upon computer power to carry out their normal business functions.

The driving force of computers is of course software, or the programs and systems that cause computers to perform useful work. As the computer era matures, the volume of software and the cost of developing and maintaining it are becoming critical parameters. Each year major corporations find themselves with expanding software staffs. Large corporations also find themselves the owners of enormous production libraries of aging and unstable applications.

In 1988, software is on the critical path leading to the successful deployment of computers for strategic and business purposes. But for the entire history of the computer era, software has lagged behind hardware in terms of economic understanding. Only since 1979 has it been possible to measure software productivity in economic terms and start dealing with software as a controllable business function. The pivotal invention was the creation of the Function Point metric by A. J. Albrecht of IBM and the discoveries subsequently derived from the use of that metric.

The standard economic definition of productivity is: "Goods or services produced per unit of labor and expense." The problem with applying economic productivity to software was that from 1943 through 1979 there was never a standard definition of exactly what "goods or services" was the output of a software development project.

As a surrogate for an acceptable economic output unit, software producers tried to use "lines of source code" as the unit of measure for software productivity, with disastrous consequences.

Most software managers and executives defined productivity as either "lines of source code produced per staff month" or "cost per source line developed." The natural assumption with productivity metrics is that as improvements in productivity occur that they will be reflected in the metric. This turned out not to be the case for "lines of source code" to the surprise of the entire industry.

In 1978, it was discovered that productivity measures expressed in source lines form paradoxically went backwards as real productivity improved. The reason for this had been known for more than 200 years by manufacturing managers, but that knowledge had not been transferred to the software community.

All manufacturing managers understand perfectly that if a manufacturing process involves a substantial percentage of fixed costs, and there is a decline in the number of units manufactured, then the cost per unit must go up.

Software, as it turns out, involves a substantial percentage of fixed or inelastic costs that are not associated with coding. When more powerful programming languages are used, the result is to reduce the number of "units" that must be produced for a given program or system, and the cost per unit will go up.

In the late 1970's, A. J. Albrecht of IBM was asked to measure the productivity of more than 20 software projects written in various languages. He knew that source line metrics would not be suitable for this task, and so he approached software measurements from a new vantage point.

He took the position that the economic output unit of software projects should be valid for all languages, and should represent topics of concern to the users of the software. In short, he wished to measure the functionality of software.

Albrecht considered that the visible external aspects of software that could be enumerated accurately consisted of five things: the inputs to the application, the outputs from it, inquiries by users, the data files that would be updated by the application, and the interfaces to other applications. Each of these five items could be measured early in the development cycle, and each would stay constant regardless of the language in which the application was coded.

In October of 1979, Albrecht first presented the results of this new software measurement technique, termed "Function Points", at a joint SHARE/GUIDE/IBM conference in Monterey, California. This marked the first time in the history of the computing era that economic software productivity could actually be measured.

The Function Point method has evolved substantially since 1979 as both Albrecht and other researchers continue their studies. In 1986, the non-profit International Function Point User Group (IFPUG) was formed to assist in transmitting data and information about this metric, and in 1987 the British government adopted a modified form of Function Points as the standard software productivity metric.

As of 1988, some 500 major corporations throughout the world are using Function Points and the number of individual projects measured with Function Points exceeds 25,000. The rate of growth of Function Point usage has been doubling each year, and the methodology is rapidly becoming the de facto world-wide standard for measuring information systems.

But Function Point usage requires some care to reach its full level of effectiveness. The counting conventions for Function Points are not completely intuitive, and unless examples and case studies are used there is a chance that errors of a significant magnitude can result in the Function Point totals.

J. Brian Dreger of Boeing is both a Function Point user and a teacher of considerable skill. He recognizes that new users of Function Points need careful guidance to become successful users, and that the human mind works best from examples and case studies.

This book is the result of Brian's successful efforts to introduce Function Points to novice users. It is clear, pragmatic, and practical in its outlook.

From 1943 until 1979, software had no effective productivity metrics at all. From 1979 to 1988, software had an effective productivity metric but a shortage of good tutorial materials to learn that metric. Now the metric and the methods of learning are moving to a new level of effectiveness.

A. J. Albrecht's invention of Function Points and their first publication in 1979 caused a revolution in software engineering. The impact of Function Points on software productivity studies may turn out to be as significant as the invention of the barometer or the mercury thermometer. For the first time in history, important factors affecting software can be measured accurately.

T. CAPERS JONES
President,
Software Productivity Research, Inc.
Cambridge, Massachusetts
Author, Consultant, and Lecturer

ACKNOWLEDGMENTS

This book would not have been possible without the help of many people, to whom I am deeply grateful:

Allan J. Albrecht of IBM, for 14 years of brilliant research and dedication as project manager to this outstanding and badly-needed methodology;

M. Kay Schimanski of Unisys Corporation (Burroughs), Lombard, Illinois, a truly extraordinary instructor—the very best of 24 fine Burroughs instructors from whom I had the pleasure of learning MIS from A to Z;

Professor Eberhard E. Rudolph of the University of Auckland and early GUIDE FPA researcher, for the on-line parts and personnel case studies requirements definition, reports, and screens; the 13-system FPA evaluation project; and artwork noticeably better than mine;

Sisters Susan Welsby and Dolores Strunk of Kansas Newman College, Wichita, Kansas, for typing this manuscript ("All we *really* wanted was to learn to use our new word processor!");

Darlene Brown, Royal Bank of Canada, Toronto, and President of the International Function Point User Group (IFPUG), for providing me complete research materials;

Brenda Dorr, Bank of Nova Scotia, Toronto, and GUIDE International, for the FPA implementation materials;

Boeing (Wichita Division) Engineering Software Training Manager Ernie R. Shoaf and 73 quality students at Boeing, Wichita State University, and Kansas Newman College, for their review of this work;

T. Capers Jones, President of Software Productivity Research, Cambridge, Massachusetts, for Figure 44 and helpful guidance on the entire book;

Ken Davis and Roger Linn of R&D Systems, Colorado Springs, for providing me the General Accounting Package ("GAP", a high-quality and versatile accounting system) Inventory Control inquiry screen and Sales Analysis reports;

Carol K. McClain of Unisys Corporation, Detroit, for the 4GL cost-benefit analysis;

Hilda V. Carpenter of National Information Systems, San Jose, California, for valuable information on ACCENT R (a state-of-the-art 4GL systems generator producing applications 20-times-faster-than-COBOL in the DEC VAX/VMS environment);

Patricia (Pat) Henry, Kimberly M. Bannon, Ed Moura, Gertrude Szyferblatt, Frances Mencarini, and Diane Spina, Prentice Hall publishing professionals of highest caliber; and

My wonderful family—Barbara, Eddy, Susan, Barbara Jo, and Paul—who gave up their time with Daddy so I could write this book (and Grandma, who looked after all of them while I did much of it!). My sincere thanks to all the above people, and my best to you, too! GOOD LUCK AND GOOD MANAGING!

1

Introduction, Function Point Identification and Classification

Traditionally, one of the most difficult aspects of a systems analyst's job has been the accurate estimation of project sizing, required development time, and end-user value. Existing productivity evaluation methods—counting either lines of code or specific coding language constructs—are useless as estimators because the programs have to be written first. Even with existing code, the disappointing and often grossly inadequate results are all too well known. Many times, better results could be achieved by using the following methods:

or, perhaps,

or, perhaps still,

```
1   REM *** PROGRAM NAME: SWAG GENERATOR ***
2   REM ***********************************************
3   REM *  BOSS ASKED ME TO ESTIMATE PROJECT VALUE &  *
4   REM *  DURATION BY END OF TODAY.   SOUNDED REAL    *
5   REM *  URGENT!  ...BEATS THE HECK OUT OF ME HOW,   *
6   REM *  THOUGH!  SURE GLAD I HAVE THIS PROGRAM!     *
7   REM ***********************************************
8   REM
10  PROJECT_DURATION = 0
20  PROJECT_DURATION = [( 13 * RND(1) ♈) ** e] * 365
30  REM  OH-MY-GOSH-I-JUST-REMEMBERED!!!
40  REM  I'VE GOT A PERFORMANCE APPRAISAL VERY SOON!!!
50  PROJECT_DURATION = PROJECT_DURATION * 3
60  REM  THERE, THAT SHOULD COVER ME NICELY!!!
70  PRINT  "TOTAL EXPECTED PROJECT DURATION = ";
            PROJECT_DURATION; "MONTHS"
80  REM  WHEW!!!  DODGED ANOTHER BULLET!!!
99  END
```

Even if these processes were consistent and accurate in their results, they cannot be taught to others; and since they were usually not only wrong but dead wrong—who needs them?

More significantly, you cannot <u>manage</u> what you cannot <u>measure</u>.

Scientific progress in every field has been heavily dependent upon the ability to take accurate measurements. Progress in all of the sciences has been significantly obliged to progress in measurement for progress [to occur] in the science itself.

But the measurement of programming has for more than 35 years been the weakest link in the whole science of software engineering. When the common metrics used for programming are explored under controlled situations, we discover three major mathematical paradoxes that have completely distorted the history of programming and concealed significant true progress:

Lines-of-code measures penalize high-level languages and often move in the wrong direction as productivity improves. They are not only difficult to apply, but ambiguous and paradoxical even when applied carefully. An entire generation of software researchers assumed incorrectly that improving productivity meant increasing the number of lines that could be developed per year, hence lowering the cost per source line.

Cost-per-defect measures penalize high-quality programs and always move in the wrong direction as quality improves.

Ratios established for programming subactivities such as design, coding, integration, or testing often move in unexpected directions in response to unanticipated factors.

These paradoxes—all caused by lines-of-code measures that penalize high-level languages and also falsely distort cost-per-defect measures—must be settled before programming and software engineering can become a precision science. They may only be settled by precision measurement, which thus becomes the most important issue as well as the most fundamental.[1]

As a result, projects were rarely completed on time, on budget, or to end-users' satisfaction. A corollary to Murphy's Law even described the value of *careful* project planning: It only takes *twice* as long to complete as expected, compared to three times for careless project planning! Also, the results were meaningless to the end user; he or she could not possibly know the business value of the new system, as may be seen on the next page.

---

[1]Jones, T. Capers, "How *Not* to Measure Programming Productivity", *Computerworld*, 13 January 1986, p. 65.

Together, these problems constitute one of the five "fundamental issues that must be resolved" to satisfy some serious concerns held by top managers nationwide about the cost-effectiveness of their data processing departments[2].

Fortunately, IBM's Allan J. Albrecht in 1979 developed (and in 1983 revised[3]) an evaluation method known as Function Point Analysis which has achieved great industry success. Function Point Analysis sizes an application from an end-user perspective instead of the technical details of the coding language. In fact, it is totally independent of all language considerations and has successfully been applied to more than 250 different languages—the 30 most common of which are presented in Figure 44. Easily learned by both end users and computer specialists, FPA accurately and reliably evaluates—to within *10%* for existing systems and *15-20%* for planned systems—

- the business value of a system to the *user*
- project size, cost, and development time
- MIS shop programmer productivity and quality
- maintenance, modification, and customization effort
- feasibility of in-house development
- fourth-generation language (4GL) implementation benefits.

[2]Jones, T. Capers, *Programmer Productivity*, McGraw-Hill, New York, 1986, p. 3.

[3]*IEEE Transactions on Software Engineering*, November 1983, pgs. 639-647.

FPA is by far the *most accurate and effective software metric ever developed*.

But one does *not* have to be a propeller-headed rocket scientist to learn or to use it. Learning this methodology will not cost you all the gold in Fort Knox and will not require from you a millennium in time. Neither will using it. Extensive studies at both IBM and Unisys have found the average overhead rate in time to be *less than 1/10 of 1%*! In the five minutes you take to get your morning cup of coffee, you can find (with uncanny accuracy!) eight to ten function points, worth an *entire month* of production!

Super! So how, then, does FPA actually work? Again, remember that FPA evaluates end-user system value; it is closely related to an application's requirements definition. A *function point* is defined as one end-user business function. Therefore, a program rated as having "x" function points delivers "x" business functions to the user. Often, the systems analyst will work directly with an end user to determine this value; this approach has achieved by far the best results—not only in Function Point Analysis, but also in user/data processing working relationships. This process requires two major steps.

1. First, business functions made available to the *user* are identified and then organized into the following five groups:

- Outputs
- Inquiries
- Inputs
- Files
- Interfaces.

Outputs are items of business information processed by the computer for the end user.

Inquiries may be considered a simple output; more precisely, they are direct inquiries into a data base or master file that look for specific data, use simple keys, require immediate response, and perform no update functions.

Inputs are items of business data sent by the user to the computer for processing and to add, change, or delete something.

Files are data stored for an application, as *logically* viewed by the user.

Interfaces are data stored elsewhere by another application but used by the one under evaluation.

This is the order in which these functions should be analyzed when designing a *new* system. (Later we shall learn that the proper evaluation order for an *existing* system undergoing maintenance or enhancement is files and interfaces *first*, then outputs, inquiries, and inputs—more on this in Chapter 5.) Readers familiar with such tools as HIPO charts and structured data flow diagrams (if you are not familiar with these, you *should* be!) will find ready use for these techniques. The context diagram "area under study" is precisely the same as the application boundary; the individual business function categories are discussed under their respective sections. The proper times to do this are as follows:

1. as soon as requirements have been well identified as defined in the Requirements Definition (Needs Analysis) Report—after approximately 5% of project duration;
2. at the end of the design phase—after approximately 80% of project duration;
3. after implementation to provide a final evaluation of user business functions and a means to analyze variances from estimates; and
4. any other time deemed necessary or beneficial under the circumstances.

But only those functions *approved* by (even if not originally or specifically *requested*) and clearly beneficial to the end user are counted; job control language and functions necessary to support technical requirements of the coding language or internal machine requirements (such as system files) are not. For example, a sorted output file would be counted, but the temporary sort file would not. As another example, when a machine is dedicated to one application and utilities provide function, only consider those utilities which are used directly by end users in place of application programs. Utilities are not to be counted on shared machines, even if they seemingly replace application programs. (However, regions and/or common areas are initialized from files when either type system is first brought up. Therefore, these areas count as files, but fields that are transparent or unavailable to the user are not counted. If they can change a flag, count them. Group the flags into logical line items of control files.) Sometimes, the distinction is not clear. For example, checkpoint files or sequential tape files converted to ISAM/VSAM for faster access may or may not be requested features, hence may or may not be counted. In this case, ask the user whether or not such features should be included—the omission may have been an oversight, and your attention to detail will be appreciated. Do not, however, include features in the function point count for which you do not have an authorizing autograph (which, in turn, ultimately depends on this: Is the user willing to pay money for this feature?). If, and only if, the omission constitutes a "vital function"—something without which the system will not fly (or even run)—*include* the feature and invoice accordingly unless the user has specifically and in writing requested its omission. Although I know there currently exists disagreement on the subject, I contend backup files and procedures *should* be included as a "vital function" and counted accordingly (as we shall see later, as a system output—not logical internal file). I know all too well the absolute chaos and feelings of utter helplessness that result from the lack of proper backup procedures when disaster strikes: I was once asked to counsel (actually, *console*, since the damage had already occurred) a customer—my *first* meeting with them (or they would assuredly have known better!)—who had experienced a disaster but who had done no backup for *more than 2 years*! Now, even though after the ship has sunk everyone knows how it *could* have been saved, I am certain that they, like smart businesspersons everywhere, would consider a good backup procedure to be cheap insurance. To settle for anything less is to settle for minimal professionalism and maximum financial risk. Again, the user will appreciate such attention to detail.

After this has been done, each business function is classified and weighted by its level of complexity—the Information Processing Function—simple, average, or complex. We shall soon learn how to do this. Extensive guidelines, refined by years of use, assure accuracy and reliability; only a few minor issues still remain undefined. Totalling all the weighted functions provides an application's total unadjusted, or raw, function point value. This figure represents a preliminary evaluation of the project's size and usefulness.

In a study of 13 applications ranging in size from 105 function points (a small system) to 2047 function points (a very large system), outputs on average contributed 24% of the total function point value; inquiries, 8%; inputs, 31%; files, 36%; and interfaces, 1%. Note, however, the wide range of values for each group:

FIGURE 1.   Summary of Function Point Distribution in 13 Applications.

Application	Function Points	Per Cent Contribution				
		Output	Inquiries	Input	Files	Interfaces
Meat Processing	654	30	7	28	35	0
Share Purchase	166	18	8	37	28	9
Corporate Accounting	2047	18	4	34	45	0
Job Costing	485	18	2	26	52	2
Utility Rates	1777	28	6	37	30	0
Work in Process	528	34	0	26	32	9
Purchased Material	108	27	0	26	29	19
Retail Parts	662	17	22	21	40	0
Wholesale Distribution	714	23	20	18	39	0
Message Switching	129	13	22	49	16	0
Teller System	604	28	12	39	21	0
Money Transfer System	105	55	0	18	7	20
Library Issue	186	48	0	31	21	0
WEIGHTED AVERAGE	628	24	8	31	36	1

These values may or may not represent your application's values. Although they may not be used as size estimators, they possibly may be used as general composition guidelines. For example, the accounting, job costing, and retail parts systems all require many and/or complex files to produce relatively little—although important—output, although the latter application does provide extensive inquiry capability. In general, an application (such as share purchase and purchased material in Figure 1) whose outputs and inquiries together do not provide at least 30% of the total system value *may* indicate underutilization of potential system business functions—that is, too little useful business information is provided compared to the amount of data which must be entered and stored. More than 31%

input or 36% files may indicate the same thing. As other examples, neither money transfer nor message switching requires extensive files, but money transfer provides exceptionally high output, while message switching requires high input. It, as do both retail parts and wholesale distribution, provides extensive inquiry capability. Finally, high interface values for purchased material and money transfer indicate that these applications depend greatly on others for much of their information.

    2. The next step, which we shall study in Chapter 3, is to adjust this raw total according to factors in the production environment, collectively referred to as the General Application Characteristics. For now, note in Figure 2 the five business function groups we have defined: outputs, inquiries, inputs, files, and interfaces. Note also the relationships between these and end users (including Operations and Auditing departments personnel, and those persons performing data entry, application inquiry, or administration functions) or other applications.

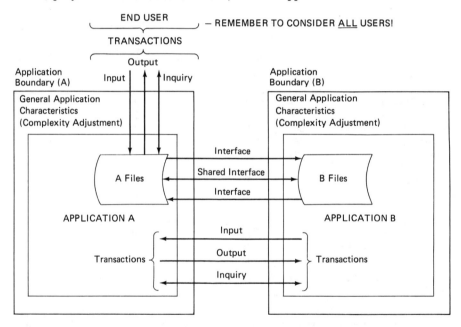

FIGURE 2.   Relationships of Users, Applications, and Business Functions.

Study the application boundary lines; while conceptually obvious, they are sometimes hard to define precisely. Remember that the application boundary is the limit of the context diagram "area under study"; it defines what your system is—and is not. Clearly, to be counted as a business function, a feature must provide some utility or benefit to the end user, whether directly through the application under study or indirectly through the adjoining (interfacing) application(s). The user must be able to see and use these business functions—or at least know they exist. From an operational standpoint, the user must know what the system can and cannot do. From an FPA standpoint, the user must know which business functions are included in the system and which are not. Only user-*required* (or *approved*) business functions are counted. These are counted as they are *logically*—not physically—implemented. That is, we are concerned with the "what" and *not* the "how" of things. Although an application is normally evaluated as a whole (IFPUG gives an alternate definition of application boundary as the logical limits of an "implemented system, the maintenance of which is managed as a unit"), there are general situations in which function points are counted in parts:

1. the application will be developed in multiple stages using multiple development projects; this situation should be considered as separate projects because it will be managed as such. A development project boundary encloses each subdivision of an application. The exchange of data between projects is included in each project's function points. The application's boundary includes all of the projects, but no function points are counted for interfaces between subdivisions of the application. When a development project is implemented as additional functionality for an existing application currently being maintained, the additional function points are added to the application in order to measure future maintenance. An exception is the interfaces between the newly-implemented functions and the existing application. These interfaces are eliminated because they are now within the expanded application boundary;

2. the application will be developed and managed as a single project, but is too big to evaluate altogether; the application may be divided into smaller parts of arbitrary size for analysis—but be careful not to double count any business functions; and

3. application code—subroutines, libraries, or IPO routines—will be brought in from existing application programs ("reused code") or purchased software. Be careful to count only those imported business functions that are either stated in the approved requirements definition report or are not stated there but actually used nonetheless, not those that take a free ride into the application boundary but do no work and provide no benefit.

IDENTIFYING AND WEIGHTING FUNCTION POINTS

We shall now learn how to count and weight function points for *your* designed application. First, *outputs* —what business information does your computer give you? (Note: the two-letter abbreviations may be translated as follows:

OT, output types	FT, file types
IT, input types	EI, external interfaces
QT, query types	

You may run across these abbreviations in other FPA articles. I have elected not to use them but include them for your convenience and cross-reference.)

OUTPUTS (OT)

You should count *each unique* user data or control output procedurally generated that leaves the application boundary. Note from Figure 2 that this includes reports and messages sent not only to the user, but also to other applications and to their users. If you are using structured analysis and design techniques ("and if not, *why* not?!!" See FitzGerald and FitzGerald for the best 100 or so pages I know on the subject—pages 50-113 and selected pages following), you would count *each* of the outputs leaving the context diagram "area under study" at the lowest (greatest detail) level of the *logical* (not physical) data flow diagram system, even if the process from which it flows is not at the data or functional (processing) primitive level. For example, an extract file sent to another application for further processing would be counted as an output, even though its contents may not be seen by a user. If the file is also printed, an additional output is counted.

An output is considered unique if:

1. it has a different format, or
2. it has the same format as another output but requires different processing logic—such as different files being accessed, different calculations made, or different processing procedures used.

It is extremely important that you understand the consequences of this definition; if you do not, you will fail to identify many user business functions. *Each* report format, totals level (control break, sub, minor, major, grand, etc.), detail (or summary) level, or different processing period should be counted *separately*. For example, an 80 column screen report contains exactly the same information as does a 132 column printer report. The screen report and printer report would each be counted as outputs because their formats differ. These examples are true even if the report has only one title and number. On the other hand, if both the screen and the printer reports were 80 (or, rarely, 132) columns, only one output would be counted because the formats are the same.

As another example, let us suppose we have a report that consists of detail lines at the top and a footing (totals) line at the bottom. We would count both the detail and the summary report as outputs. This is because different processing logic is required to total, rather than just print, report fields. It may have a different order or even different content, and will be used in different ways—perhaps by different people—from the detailed portion. (This is the Unisys position, which I support. IFPUG, however, disagrees. It contends that summary and total lines come with the territory and, therefore, are not usually counted as a separate benefit or business function.) Lead yourself not into the temptation to cram everything into one "supercomplex" output! Although all these outputs may be physically presented on one piece of paper, they logically are not alike and, therefore, must be treated separately. Now suppose this report is to be produced on a daily, a weekly, and a monthly basis. Since different processing periods require different processing logic, we would now have a total of six outputs, that is, 2 * 3. Finally, suppose this same report is to be both displayed on a screen and printed on a printer. As before, if the two formats differ, we would have 12 (= 6 * 2) outputs; if the formats were the same, we would still have six. Again, make sure you fully understand all the consequences of this rule; serious calculation errors will be made if you do not.

Where can you look for potential outputs? Besides the obvious screen or terminal and printed batch reports, the following can often be outputs:

- transaction file sent to another application
- computer output microforms (COM)—fiche, film, etc.
- picking tickets and counter slips
- bill of material
- customer invoices
- payroll or accounts payable checks
- digital or analog actuators
- automatic transactions
- punched cards or paper tape
- digital lines or magnetic stripes
- floppy disk transactions
- user screen messages
- user-maintained table or file (for maintenance)
- user application controls (including switch responses)
- tape transaction
- query language outputs not an inquiry
- voice responses
- graphs, charts, graphics, CAD, and CAE
- backup file.

Then, count as *one* output *each* uniquely formatted or processed portion of the following that is both used and approved by the user (note that some of these descriptions, and those presented in the other four business function groups, overlap to account for the different perspectives on the subject readers are likely to possess):

- formatted printout of master or transaction file not claimed elsewhere by a specific report
- backup file; even though produced internally, its real value is that it makes its usual home elsewhere and thus would hopefully be available "out of the bullpen" if the primary production version were wiped out—truly a "vital function" in time of disaster
- ad-hoc report generator or DBMS report writer template; if this tool is provided it is impossible to count function points for all possibilities, and you must settle the issue by crediting the application with one complex output—a most reasonable solution
- screen output—one per unique format, detail level, processing logic, etc. (unless an inquiry response)
- batch printed report—same as for screens
- batch run control report—both counts and amounts
- batch error report
- single-level sorts on a different key, only if reformatting is required—such as moving a sort field to the first column of the report. For example, a report that breaks on a state change is considered one report. If data is extracted to produce separate state reports in the same report layout, it is still considered to be the same report. If, however, data is rearranged and requires additional processing logic to produce the new format, it is considered to produce additional user functions which are counted accordingly. As another example, suppose a second report is produced which duplicates another, except that it eliminates some data. Since it satisfies a different user function, it is considered to be another output, but perhaps of lesser complexity
- each different order, in different reports, of a multi-level (by x, by y, by z) file sort if appropriately re-formatted
- each different total level of a report—column, control group, minor, major, grand, etc. (but please refer again to earlier IFPUG counterpoint)
- each different processing period for a report—daily, weekly, monthly, quarterly, yearly, etc. (but please refer again to earlier IFPUG counterpoint)
- control totals report (both counts and amounts)
- audit trail or checklist report
- check register
- selection menu screen output with save capability
- start screen output—like the initialization of conversational processing
- summary/ending screen output—like EOJ (end-of-job) confirmation
- MICR/OCR scan lines—one output per embedded format
- detail screen output
- user-accessible report file

- user-maintained table or file; more than one output is possible (and usually + 3 inputs and 1 inquiry as well)
- messages to operator (1 per general *format* if standalone; otherwise include each message field as 1 data item for complexity classification purposes if the messages are integrated into output format)—both information, confirmation, and error unless a single message, a simple acknowledgement of the entry transaction, or unless requires no processing logic other than an edit check. However, calculated fields displayed on an input screen are each counted separately as an output—for example, the number of edit records accepted or master records updated. If counted, the error message references either one file (if a user-maintained error code-to-text table is used) or none. If different edit rules exist depending on the path selected by a previous screen (for example, a previous screen requested a password which in turn determined what you can do), only one screen may be counted, notwithstanding the different paths
- data, function, or control transactions to other applications
- screen both output and input (+ 1 input)—unless an inquiry
- output file of automatic data or processed transaction records sent to another application (+ 1 interface, discussed later)
- query language outputs (unless an inquiry)—1 per output
- report file passed to another application for print, forms, and/or graphics imaging (+ 1 interface for receiving program)
- interpretive language used by application for report generation capabilities; count each verb or keyword as 1 data item for complexity classification purposes.

However, do *not* count the following as outputs:

- those introduced only because of the technology used[4]
- titles, prompts, column headers, or page numbers
- paging capabilities or "next format" fields—these are counted as end-user efficiency characteristics
- *individual* messages (information, confirmation, and error) if the general standalone message format was already counted above, or if they are integrated with output as one data item referenced

[4]I cannot believe it, but this statement has been dropped from the official GUIDE International GPP-134 rulebook; its editor joins this author in wanting it re-instated. FPA is supposed to "look at the application from the point of view of the USER" (IFPUG). The user wants functionality, not technology—unless, and only unless, technology provides functionality. But no business functions are stated or implied in the situation referenced—in it, outputs have been created only as a by-product of the technology used and may not even be desired, let alone requested or approved! There would otherwise be a great temptation to fill one's toybox with all the "latest and greatest" toys—whose value to the end user would possibly be minimal at best. Eventually, I think this statement will be re-instated; but for now, don't count outputs introduced *only* because of the technology used.

- single or multiple-level sorts on a different key or key order unless the format is changed accordingly; unless the format is changed, count only one version of the report because sorting by name, for example, does not require different processing logic from sorting by SSN
- output files of unprocessed transaction records; these will be counted as inputs and possibly also as interfaces by the receiving application
- output files of processed master file records; these are counted as interfaces and as logical internal files
- output responses of inquiries; these will be classified as inquiries
- output responses of menu selection; these will be classified as inquiries
- outputs in the same format (and logic) as one already counted for a different media or output device (screen or printer), or report files spooled for later printing on either the same or a different device
- repeat screens, printed pages, or detail lines
- selection menu screen with save capability; this is counted as 1 input + 1 inquiry
- file dumps; formatted file printouts, however, are counted
- other outputs not approved by the user.

Now that we have found these functions (and discarded those it would be cheating to claim!), we need to classify them. Note from the following chart that this depends on two things—the number of files (to be defined shortly under "FILES") referenced, or accessed, and the number of data items (variables or "buckets"— *possibly* fields if other unseen items are not involved) referenced. A data item need neither be printed nor stored in an organized data set, file, or table—it only need be referenced (accessed or used) to count. Note that only data items actually referenced are counted; data items residing in the same file or data set but *not* referenced are *not* counted. No game participation credit for remaining "on the bench"! However, a data item may be counted only once per output, regardless of the number of times it actually appears or is used in calculations. This notwithstanding, data transformed to make it easier to read and understand counts as one data item referenced for each such method used. For example, if "net pay" may print as "$****200.00", "200.00", and "two hundred and no/one-hundredths dollars" in various places on the check, each conversion counts as 1 data item, for a total of 3 data items for net pay in this example . A report column represents one data item if the data item is only printed and not calculated by the application program. However, if a report column contains calculated or code-converted data, *all contributing data items* must also be counted; the report column is always included as a separate data item (in addition to its contributors) even if it is the result of calculations made on two (or more) other report columns. Data items that result from calculations or code-conversion are always more difficult to identify because they are not necessarily contained in logical internal files nor even displayed to or seen by the user. For example, a column in which a salesperson's name is printed

printed is one data item because it is printed without any calculation being done. But a column containing the year-to-date average monthly sales value for a single product references three data items—total YTD sales quantity (for this product), product sales price, and current month number; note that only the first two data items will likely be stored in a file or data set—that the current month number will be provided by the system clock does not take away the fact it is still a data item for FPA counting purposes. Also understand that the number of detail lines produced has absolutely *no* effect on the complexity classification. This is determined *only* by the number of files and data items referenced, not the number of detail lines printed. In fact, a one-line report referencing at least 4 files and 20 data items would be complex, but a 1000-page report referencing only 1 file and 19 data items would still be simple.

FIGURE 3. Outputs.

	1 - 5 data items referenced	6 - 19 data items referenced	20 or more data items referenced
0 or 1 file(s) referenced	Simple (4)	Simple (4)	Average (5)
2 or 3 files referenced	Simple (4)	Average (5)	Complex (7)
4 or more files referenced	Average (5)	Complex (7)	Complex (7)

From this chart it may be seen that 26 data items accessed from two files would be classified as complex and given a weighting factor of 7; 19 data items from three files would be classified as average and given a weighting factor of 5; and five data items from three files would be classified as simple and given a weighting factor of 4. Remember that referenced items do not need to be organized into a data set, file, or table; up to 19 COBOL 77-level items could be accessed and themselves be classified as a simple output—or average if more files or items were used. Also remember that each file found later should be provided a formatted print option—not a mere file dump—and so should at least be classified as simple or average, as appropriate, regardless of what other uses it may have.

In earlier FPA handbooks, you might have noticed something called "Additional Factors," whose purpose was to "adjust the result up or down not more than one level." Because such factors, along with many others, are included in the General Application Characteristics (Complexity Adjustment), they should *NOT* be used here because you would be double counting, introducing subjective factors into what should only be objectively numeric, and implying an unrealistically high impact on the application. These same comments also apply to the other four business function groups: DO *NOT* USE THEM!

To review, counting (raw) output business functions consists of two related steps—identification and classification. Make sure you understand how this is done before you continue; other business function groups are done precisely the same way. With a little practice, this process will become easy. Until then, count, re-count, and count again. The main cause of inaccuracy, particularly in the early stages of development, is overlooking indicated business functions. But never assume that the documentation provided you is complete. It never is. Expect and probe for more functions; the user will appreciate this attention to detail. Brainstorm. Work with others. Don't omit any functions—each one costs you 4 to 7 points. It is more important to *list* a function than to *classify* it—but try not to miss on either. Even though it means only one or two points, these can be important, especially when you are only one or two data items away from the next higher complexity level; no longer can the "additional factors" push you over the goal line! As on your tax form, do not cheat—but claim all that is properly due you. Remember that outputs in the 13 applications studied earlier on average contributed about 24% of the function point total; if they do not provide a similar value in your application portfolio, you may not be getting full value from your system, or you may have missed some business functions. Depending on which, if either, of these is the case, do what you need to do.

Normally, we would next evaluate inquiries. To do this, though, we first need to know how to evaluate inputs. This is because inquiries are combinations of both inputs and outputs; only one value, the greater of the two, is applied. So we shall now consider *inputs*—what business data must your computer have to process information for you?

INPUTS (IT)

You should count *each unique* user data or control input that enters the application boundary *and also updates* (adds to, changes, or deletes from) a logical internal file, data set, table, or independent data item. Please return to Figure 2 and note that this includes not only inputs entered directly by the user as transactions, but also input files and transactions received from other applications. If you are using structured analysis and design techniques, you would count *each* of the inputs entering the context diagram "area under study" at the *lowest* (greatest detail) level of the logical data flow diagram system, even if the process into which it flows is not at the data or functional (processing) primitive level. For example, an extract file received from another application for further processing would be counted as an input even though its contents may not be seen by a user. If the file is also printed, an additional input is counted.

An input is considered unique if:

1. it has a different format, or
2. it has the same format as another input (for example, screen appearances are identical) but requires different processing logic—such as different func-

tions being performed (the same entities are modified in different ways) or a different logical internal file or data item is modified.

As was the case with outputs, it is extremely important that you understand the consequences of this definition; if you do not, you will again fail to identify many user business functions. This is true even though inputs are generally not as difficult to identify and classify as are outputs. Still, "different processing logic" may cause difficulties with input identification as it did with output. Usually this term means that different files, data sets, data stores, etc. are modified but it can also mean that the *same* files, data sets, data stores, etc. are modified but in different ways.

For example, suppose we have two input screens, each with the same format but different processing logic. We would count each screen as a separate input. But if the same two screens had identical processing logic, only one would be counted as an input. The same would be true for repeated screens—only the first would be counted.

As another example, suppose we have a screen whose function is to update a file or data set. Since each of the three update functions (add, change, and delete) requires different processing logic, we would have three inputs, not just one. Every other file would also have three inputs, as well as one output (the formatted file printout) and one inquiry (a quick-browse capability). Again, make sure you fully understand all the consequences of this rule; serious calculation errors will be made if you do not.

Where can you look for potential inputs? Besides the obvious screen data entry, the following can often be inputs:

- mouse
- MICR documents
- OCR documents
- automatic teller machine (ATM)
- automatic transactions
- tape transaction
- floppy disk transactions or transaction files from another application
- key-to-storage files or keyed document
- punched cards or paper tape
- digital or analog sensors
- magnetic stripes
- voice inputs
- switches
- light pens
- touch-sensitive screens
- touch-tone telephones (or emulators)

- bar code readers
- optical scanning devices or digitizers
- special-function key process
- user-maintained table or file (for maintenance)
- query language inputs that are not inquiries
- user application controls (including switch inputs).

Then, count as *one* input *each* uniquely formatted or processed portion of the following:

- security password or collection of conversational screens to access *application* (not merely log onto the machine)
- screen data input (include acknowledgement response message as 1 data item in classification)
- screen function input (1 per function—add, change, and delete); each of these functions would be separately evaluated for complexity
- data set or master file (3 per file or data set)
- new master file created after sequential update process; given an old (already counted) master file to be updated by a transaction tape (which counts as either 1 input or 1 interface), the new master file produced should be counted as a new logical internal file for this application and possibly also as an interface if exported elsewhere
- inquiry followed by update input (+ 1 inquiry)—"tell me what's in the data base, then let me change the fields I want to change"
- MICR scan line—as with the OCR scan line, 1 input per embedded format, or if different processing logic
- OCR scan line, wand, or bar code reader
- other machine-readable input forms
- credit card, ATM card, security badge, etc. magnetic stripe inputs
- two input screens, each with same format and processing logic as the other: count the *collection* together as *one*, not two, input
- as above, but with different processing logic (1 per screen)—this also means that a subsequent screen with both the same format and the same functions offered as a previous screen count as a separate input if the data items, or the files in which they are stored, vary from the previous update's data structure in any way
- automatic data or transaction file (+ 1 interface, discussed later, only if data conversion is required); one input is counted for each different type transaction contained within the file (but count only if actually used), or for each contributing file format if input files are concatenated (appended, or joined) and separate processing logic is required for each

- user-maintained table or file; more than one input (add, change, delete) is possible and, in fact, is usual (also + 1 output, 1 inquiry)
- data, function, or control transactions from other applications (+ 1 interface, discussed later)
- selection menu screen input with save capability (+ 1 inquiry)
- interpretive language used by application for file update capabilities; count each verb or keyword as 1 data item for complexity classification purposes
- control information for report selection
- user application control input—sign on, sign off, password, and switch settings—each field represents 1 data item
- query language inputs (unless an inquiry)—1 per input
- update function that is a component of a report or query facility
- screen both input (updates) and output (reports) (+ 1 output)—unless an inquiry; be sure to count *each* input function provided and *each* output function provided if more than one of each exist.

However, do *not* count the following as inputs:

- those introduced only because of the technology used (see earlier discussion under outputs)
- incoming master files; these are interfaces (and also logical internal files if shared or internally updated)
- automatic data loading by another program, or of the data base, since this constitutes internal file transfer whose inputs were counted at the time of initial data entry
- machine (as opposed to application) logon security procedures; these are standard in a mainframe environment and often nonexistent in a micro
- alternate input with the same processing logic as the primary input—for example, entering "ADD", "add", "A", or "a" to add a new record counts as only 1 input, not 4
- special-function key or light pen duplicate of screen already counted as an input
- *individual* messages (information, confirmation, and error; these are included as part of the basic input function and count each message field as 1 data item for complexity classification purposes)
- input portions of inquiries; these only direct the data search. They cannot update data and will be classified as inquiries
- additional types of input media for the same processing logic; count only 1 media but not the other(s)—for example, both a data entry screen and punched cards are provided for a series of transactions, but only 1 media type may be counted because format and processing logic are the same for both

- repeat screens or screen input (unless have different processing logic)—this would occur if not all data fits on 1 screen and needs another
- menu screens (count entire menu collection as 1 inquiry)
- backup input with the same processing logic as the primary input—such as a batch file which reapplies on-line transactions already counted
- implied inquiries that are part of an input function (initial display of data) are not counted as inquiries; however, the display fields are counted as data items for complexity classification purposes
- data screen template produced in a second language—as was the case with outputs, this will be accounted for in the production environment complexity factors portion
- other inputs not approved by the user.

Now that we have identified and recorded only valid input functions, we need to classify them—in a manner similar to output. Note from the chart below that this depends on exactly the same two things (with *no* "additional factors" tiebreakers)—number of files and of data items referenced—but that the row, column, and weighting factor values are all different. Each screen field, document field, directives field (for example, to perform an alpha or soundex search), parameter, functional command, screen-to-screen command transfer line (count 1 data item for each entry the line can, though not necessarily will, have at any one time), or input file field represents one and only one data item, as was *not* the case with outputs; input complexity classification is otherwise done precisely the same way as was output classification. Only those data items actually updated by the transaction should be included, not the total number resident in the logical file.

FIGURE 4.   Inputs.

	1 - 4 data items referenced	5 - 15 data items referenced	16 or more data items referenced
0 or 1 file(s) referenced	Simple (3)	Simple (3)	Average (4)
2 files referenced	Simple (3)	Average (4)	Complex (6)
3 or more files referenced	Average (4)	Complex (6)	Complex (6)

Be certain to identify all applicable inputs. Remember that they may occur in multiple places, especially when more than one input device—terminals, readers, scanners, etc.—is used, or when files are input from tape or disk. Note, too, as was the case with output that referenced data items do not need to be organized into a data set, file, or table; input items can also update COBOL 77-level items. Finally, remember that each file found later should be provided full update capability—add, change, and delete—so should at least be classified as simple or average, as appropriate, regardless of what other uses it may have.

As was the case with output, and is the case for each of the five business function groups, counting input business functions consists of two related steps— identification and classification. Do not omit any functions in any business function group! Each input missed costs you 3 to 6 points, and each misclassification costs you 1 or 2. Be extra careful and consider other possible input fields or sources when close to the next higher complexity level. For the 13 applications studied earlier, inputs on average contributed about 31% of the function point total. Your systems, of course, will probably differ from this figure; if they provide significantly more, you may be capturing some useless or underutilized information. Either identify its use as an output or internal data structure, find a use, or discard it.

We shall now consider *inquiries.* As you recall, they combine features of both inputs and outputs.

INQUIRIES (QT)

You should count *each unique* input/output combination in which the on-line user-defined input causes and generates an immediate on-line output. Please return to Figure 2 and note that inquiries may be provided to or from other applications as well as end users, even though the former type may never be seen directly by a user because the output portion is sent back to the requesting *application,* not to the user. For example, responding to another application's request for a single product's cost or current selling price would count as an inquiry under this definition.

An inquiry is considered unique if:

1. it has a format different from others in *either* its input or output portions, or
2. it has the same format, both input and output, as another inquiry but requires different processing logic in *either.*

Earlier we learned another definition of an inquiry; we discovered that for function point counting purposes, it is a direct inquiry into a data base or master file that:

1. uses *simple keys* to retrieve specific data—that is, a *single* record or group of related records, not a range;

2. requires *immediate response*[5] (as defined by the user); and

3. performs *no update* functions—it cannot add, change, or delete records, only inquire on them; data entered only directs the search but changes nothing. Note that calculations may be performed as long as they neither update files nor unreasonably degrade response time.

Together, these two definitions will help us sort out inquiries from outputs. For example, suppose we want to find out about Air Boeing Express Flight #73. This would be an inquiry because it uses a simple key, provides an immediate response, and performs no update functions to tell us such information as departure city and time, arrival city and time, number of stops, etc. On the other hand, suppose we want to find out about all flights leaving New York between 9:00 a.m. and 10:00 a.m. for Los Angeles. This would not be an inquiry under this definition; even though no updates would be performed, all necessary information is readily available, and response may still be "immediate," the range in both time and in airline companies makes the key no longer simple. And if any of these three rules is violated, as was the simple-key rule here, the "inquiry" becomes one (possibly more) input and one (possibly more) output. This rule may be extended to evaluate a major query facility's or report generator language's benefits. Unlike an inquiry, which is a direct search for specific data, a query facility (or language) provides an organized and structured collection of inputs and outputs which makes possible many different types of inquiry, often using many keys, operations, and calculations. Those responses that meet the definition of "inquiry" provided here should be identified as such; those that do not, including those provided by the query facility, should be identified as inputs and outputs, as appropriate. To review, inquiries use simple keys to look for specific data, require immediate response, and perform no update functions.

Where can you look for potential inquiries? Try these:

- user inquiry/display with no file or other logical entity update (not all will qualify)
- transaction file leaving the application boundary if this is accessible to the on-line user

---

[5]"immediate response (or output)" is sometimes *misunderstood* to mean that inquiries require less than one-second response time and must return information only to the screen from which the input was entered. Not necessarily true. What it really means is this: from a *logical* standpoint, the output response can be made available *immediately* because it uses only information currently "in stock" (or rush-order deliverable) in logical internal files, rather than data that requires *extensive* searches or calculations as discussed in requirement #3; some people contend any data value or format manipulation at all (even sorting or merging) causes the apparent inquiry response to become an output, but we shall soon see why this point is actually moot and why it would be too restrictive if it were not. Also, the output portion need *not* go back to the screen from which its input request was entered (although this is certainly the most common situation), but instead may go to a printer as long as it is not first placed in a batch queue. If this happens, the "inquiry" becomes one input and one output.

- selection menu screen (all menu screens together count as 1 inquiry)
- help screen or information message.

Then, count as *one* inquiry *each* uniquely formatted or processed portion of any of the following that is both used and approved by the user and also meets the key-response-update rule:

- on-line input and on-line output with no update
- on-line inquiry into a transaction file leaving the application boundary
- inquiry followed by update input (+ 1 input)—"tell me what's in the data base, then let me change the fields I want to change"
- help screen or information message input and output. For a help screen, the number of data items referenced is equal to the number of fields for which help is available; for a message screen, each message field is counted as 1 data item for complexity classification purposes
- selection menu screen input and output (entire collection counts as 1); the number of data items referenced is the total number of menu selection options or possible input screens for the entire system. If the menu is actually a free-form entry line with various set positions for command or data entry, the number of data items referenced is equal to the maximum number of fields that can be entered on this line. Note that menus, unlike most inquiries, are highly input-oriented
- selection menu screen input with save capability (+ 1 input)
- user-maintained table or file (usually there are also + 3 inputs, 1 output)
- interpretive language used by the application for inquiry capabilities; evaluate both input and output component using rules specified under the respective business function group and select whichever value is greater
- inquiry (only) portions of a major query facility or language; count its output and input facilities under the appropriate section elsewhere.

However, do *not* count the following as inquiries:

- those introduced only because of technology used (see earlier discussion under outputs)
- apparent inquiries that violate the key-response-update rule; count as one (or more) inputs and one (or more) outputs
- apparent inquiries that do not have both a valid input and a valid output combination; count as either one (or more) input or one (or more) output, but not both—and appreciate that the user benefit of this may be questionable

- command line screen-to-screen transfer capability; this is considered to be included within basic screen input and output capabilities and increases the data-items-referenced count for inputs complexity classification purposes
- other inquiries not approved by the user.

Now that we know what is, and is not, a valid inquiry, how do we classify them? Note from the chart below that it consists of two parts. The top part is the part we saw earlier when classifying outputs, and the bottom part is what we just saw when classifying inputs. This combined chart is absolutely no different from either of these (except for one thing: A standalone input by definition *updates* a data store, file, data set, table, and the like, but the input portion of an inquiry only directs the search and *never* updates). This is because an inquiry is classified first by evaluating input and output individually, precisely as we have done before (it does not matter which is done first[6]), then comparing the numeric complexity value of one portion with the other and selecting whichever is greater. As with the component parts of input and output, inquiries have *no* "additional factors" tiebreakers.

FIGURE 5.   Inquiries.

Output Part:	1 - 5 data items referenced	6 - 19 data items referenced	20 or more data items referenced
0 or 1 file(s) referenced	Simple (4)	Simple (4)	Average (5)
2 or 3 files referenced	Simple (4)	Average (5)	Complex (7)
4 or more files referenced	Average (5)	Complex (7)	Complex (7)

Input Part:	1 - 4 data items referenced	5 - 15 data items referenced	16 or more data items referenced
0 or 1 file(s) referenced	Simple (3)	Simple (3)	Average (4)
2 files referenced	Simple (3)	Average (4)	Complex (6)
3 or more files referenced	Average (4)	Complex (6)	Complex (6)

[6]Note, however, that the number of data items referenced in the output portion is only by co-incidence the same as the number of data items referenced in the input portion; usually it will be greater. Similarly, the files referenced for each may also be different—in both number and purpose. Some files will validate the data entered, whereas others will gather the data for the output portion.

For example, suppose an inquiry consists of a simple input (value 3) and a simple output (value 4). The inquiry classification weighting factor would be the greater of the two values, or 4. Now suppose the same output required an average input. In this case, the inquiry classification weighting factor would still be 4; it does not matter which portion—input or output—is selected. However, most inquiries will be counted as either simple or average outputs. Since the greater of two values is selected, an inquiry can clearly never be 3; and because of the key-response-update rule, it is unlikely to be complex (6 or 7). In earlier FPA articles, what I believe to be an oversight forced *all* inquiries to be weighted the same as inputs for counting purposes; maybe this was intended to maintain symmetry in the counting worksheets—but I have overcome that, too. Whatever the cause or reason, it makes no sense at all to weight inquiries the same as inputs; it partially contradicts the "select which is greater" rule and values what would otherwise (in most cases) be an output of value 4-5-7 as a weaker input of value 3-4-6, reduced output processing complexity notwithstanding—if the output portion stood alone, it would be counted accordingly, and the addition of the input search variable(s) makes the situation more complex, not less.

To review, counting inquiry business functions consists of two steps:

1. identification; (note that those failing the key-response-update test, and those not containing both a valid input and a valid output portion, should be listed under inputs and outputs, as appropriate, not inquiries)
2. classification; the input classification is compared with the output classification and the greater of the two is selected. Usually this value will be 4 or 5, rarely 6 or 7, and never 3.

Do not omit counting any inquiry! Each one missed costs you at least 4 or 5 points, and each one misclassified can sometimes cost you 1 or 2 (misclassifying an average input as simple does no harm). Most inquiry misclassification errors occur when an average output is classified as simple. Remember that in our 13-application study, inquiries on average contributed about 8% of the function point totals but may provide more or less—even nothing.

We shall now consider the heart of any business application, *files*—what business data and information does your computer store in its warehouse?

FILES (FT)

You should count *each* major *logical* group of user data or control information (subject to content type limitations to be described shortly) maintained entirely within the application boundary. Please return to Figure 2 and note that logical internal files (including both logical files and logical data groupings within a data base) consist only of those *logical* (not physical) data sets, files, or tables which perform all capture, generation, use, maintenance, and storage functions entirely within the application boundary and are somehow available to users by way of outputs, inquiries, inputs, and/or interfaces. However, note well the fact that Function Point Analysis further distinguishes between two types of files: files with temporary transactions and files with logical records of more lasting, permanent data. Even though both kinds of data are physically stored in files, only the latter is counted as being a "logical" file for FPA counting purposes; as we shall soon see, this distinction also affects how we identify and classify interfaces. Only stores of *permanent* data are viewed as logical files. The following terms are often used to describe such logical files: "master file," "updated records," "reference files," "persistent data," "status," "record," and "historical data." When used and maintained within the application, classify them as logical internal files. When shared between applications, they are classified as both interfaces as well as logical internal files.

Transactions, on the other hand, are considered to be events that trigger changes or updates to logical internal files; they are *not* classified as files themselves. The following terms are used to describe transactions: "event," "transaction," "transient data," "stimulus," "trigger," and "update data." A print file is considered to be an output, not a logical internal file, and is further classified the same as a transaction file if exported to another application for final assembly—more on this later. A transaction file can be classified as an input if it is read to process or update data in a logical internal file. Each unique type of processing (add, change, or delete) counts as 1 input. A transaction file can be an interface or an output if it transfers update transactions to another application, in which case the receiving application would count the transactions as an input. It might also be counted as an interface, as will be discussed in the next section.

If you are using structured analysis and design techniques, each internal (within the context diagram "area under study") data store created will contain *at least one* logical internal file; this is because *several* distinct and unique entities may comprise the data store and *each* be counted as a logical internal file, and also because there may be more than one key by which the file can be accessed. If any of these functions is performed outside the application boundary, the apparent logical internal file becomes an external interface, which we shall discuss in the next section. For FPA counting purposes, only files must reside and do business entirely within the context diagram "area under study"; all other business function groups must pass through this boundary, one way or the other, to be counted.

Again note well the emphasis on logical as opposed to physical files. We must remember that Function Point Analysis is concerned with evaluation of user business functions. The user probably does not care how these files are physically organized; rather, he or she is more interested in what useful information they contain and can readily produce. To the user, *each* such (logical) collection of information is a "file." Accordingly, *each* access method or path—that is, each key or data base view—is counted as one logical internal file. *MAKE ABSOLUTELY CERTAIN YOU UNDERSTAND THIS!* For example, suppose we have one physical file that contains two different, user-accessible keys. We would count two different logical internal files because each path requires or presents different information, or uses a different format. More specifically, let this physical file be a customer master file. One door into this file is, say, customer number; this key, or path, would be counted as one logical internal file. Another door into this file is, say, customer name; this would count as another. Should it? Of course. Just think of the fun you would have if customer number were the only way you could search a 100,000 record file—and you did not know the number and could not find it! Clearly, organizing information in this manner is useful to the end user because the information now needed is available how needed; the user need not waste valuable time searching for and sorting information. Instead, this information can be used directly for better and faster business decisions. Therefore, counting each file key as a separate logical internal file is highly appropriate.[7]

Similarly, each logical user view into a data base is also counted as one file; a *view* gets together all the information (subject to security constraints—"no need, no read") associated with one function, either input or output, into one group of data (and corresponding operations on these data items) customized for that user. So is each access path within that view. Logical data base views provide not only the organizing benefits of file keys described above, but also a simple yet highly effective security mechanism to protect your organization's vital information assets. Views are user benefits and should be counted accordingly. Suppose a data base employs five different logical views for 26 users. We would count five logical internal files.

It is essential you understand this! Extremely serious errors will be made if you do not. Not only does a logical internal file provide the most "electoral votes" of any business function group (and what politician wants to lose California?), but it also takes along for a ride three inputs (add, change, and delete capabilities), one output (formatted printout of itself), and one inquiry (quick-browse capability)—at least a whopping 17 points in add-ons alone! (We shall soon see that the file itself provides 7, 10, or 15.) Don't lose points!

Where can you look for potential files? Not over or at the end of the rainbow—instead, try these:

- data bases—1 per logical view or access path
- master files—1 per key collection
- other logical internal files unless temporary or needed only to meet a program's, language's, computer's, or other file's needs

---

[7]Similarly, if a given input does three different things—say add, change, and delete—then the data updated, even if it overlaps, may be looked at as three different groups for FPA input counting purposes. However, the different collections of data items for each of these input functions do *not* themselves constitute a different logical internal file—only multiple keys can provide this.

- user-maintained table for data—tax rates, shipping rates, messages, states, etc.
- batch sequential processing control file
- user query file
- cross-reference indexes, including message table
- user-maintained ISAM/VSAM index file (must not be system-maintained). Note that this represents a *physical*, not logical, implementation and as such would ordinarily be disregarded by FPA.

Then, count as *one* logical internal file *each* major logical group of user data or control information within the application boundary:

- master file—1 per key collection. But if what is called a "master file" is only read by this application and in no way updated, then it is actually only 1 or more interface files, not a logical internal file; if, however, it is both read and updated in this application, then it is a logical internal file in this application (+ 1 interface if shared or sent elsewhere)
- logical collection or entity of data as seen by the user. Logical internal files are unique groupings of data that offer a special function from a user's perspective. For example, a data base is a logical grouping of a user's data. If data from multiple hierarchical or network segments is extracted into a flat file, the extracted file is also counted as a logical internal file. So is the resulting table in a relational data base join operation. However, if the extracted file is sorted, the sorted output file is not counted (unless substantially reformatted—and then as an *output*) because it is the same logical grouping of data; only the sequence is changed. For you statisticians, we are counting combinations, not permutations. As was the case with outputs, different time frames denote separate business functions—for example, a system which has a daily master file and a monthly consolidation of the dailies would count *both* the consolidation and (one) daily master (we are assuming a user-approved value in a standalone daily master, not just transaction, file) files as separate files—but do not force unnatural and non-customary units of time just to "roll up the score"!
- internal data store—one per component entity per key collection and applicable combination of processing switch settings (if used)
- file keys (or flat file sequence control fields)—1 per key collection
- data base logical user views—1 per view; in a relational data base, count joins only when they are necessary to satisfy an approved user requirement. The number of relationships/record types referenced is the number of relational tables accessed to create that view with a join operation

- data base access paths within views—1 per path (including secondary) if user approved[8]
- logical internal files generated or maintained by the application; within a system, a file created by one process and passed to another is counted as a logical internal file, not an interface, provided it is not just a temporary or work file, and the user requirements indicated a need for it. If it is just a processing by-product or a design consideration only, do not count it as either. A file created by one process and passed to another for printing, forms, and/or graphics imaging is normally counted as 1 output. If significant integration is required by this application to process the file, count it as an interface and an output; if the receiving application needs to do the formatting work, count both one input and one interface, and claim the final finished product as well. We shall see more on this under "INTERFACES"
- files or data sets accessible to the user through passwords, keywords, or parameters
- file or data set sent to or shared with other application(s) (+ 1 interface)
- user-maintained table or file (+ 3 input, 1 output, and 1 inquiry at least)
- sequential batch application data or control file
- each contributing input file that was concatenated (combined) into one because of like record formats, but *only* when different processing logic is required and multiple versions of the same format and logic are not double-counted

[8]Even though hierarchical data bases are not even yesterday's technology (they're the day's before!), the following considerations are provided for evaluation in a hierarchical data base environment: Each segment of a hierarchical data base counts as a record type for classification purposes. Only those fields within each segment that are actually used may be counted. All segments below the root segment of a hierarchical data base have logically concatenated keys. The user view consists of a complete path (including the root segment) of such a data base. Truncations of a complete path of a hierarchical data base do not count as additional user views. They are merely sub-sets of the more complete user view. When any segments are accessed by logical paths of secondary indexes, the resultant user views are considered to be separate structures. Count only the user views that are based on user requirements and not those that are there because the implementation made them available. When hierarchical data bases contain segments for technological reasons, such a segment (no-key segments, fragmentation of a field into multiple levels for performance considerations, etc.) should be considered as part of the parent segment with the keys concatenated and not counted separately.

When two or more physical files have the same key, they are considered to be a single user view. The sequence by which data is entered provides unique user views. A concatenated key consisting of FIELD-A and FIELD-B in that order provides a different user view from FIELD-B and FIELD-A in that order. User access (as well as approval) must be provided for the data structures in order to qualify. (A file sorted into a different sequence in order to produce reports whose parameters are not user-controlled does not count. But a file sorted into a different sequence and made available for user inquiries does count.) Finally, if a single segment of a complex data base is accessed for all transactions (for example, a name and address), it is functionally the same as a flat file. If multiple segments are accessed, the single segment is counted as any other segment.

- new master file created after sequential update process; given an old (already counted) master file to be updated by a transaction tape (which counts as either 1 input or 1 interface), the new master file produced should be counted as a new logical internal file for *this* application and possibly also as an interface if exported elsewhere
- all other valid files not otherwise claimed (+ 3 input, 1 output, and 1 inquiry per file).

However, do *not* count the following as logical internal files:

- those introduced only because of the technology used (see earlier discussion under outputs); logical groups of data that are physically stored in smaller subdivisions only for ease-of-use reasons count as only one logical internal file, not several
- files all of whose functions are not completely internal (specifically, *back-up files*—these are *outputs*)
- files maintained by another application
- files not accessible to the user through input, output, inquiry, or interface processes
- hard-coded information not directly maintainable by or available to the user
- transaction or print files; these are inputs or outputs, and possibly also interfaces
- files sorted in different order from or appended to another file already counted; for example, to count month-end totals as a separate logical file when they are added to year-to-date totals (already counted) would be wrong
- internal system files—work files, intermediate files, temporary sort files, or ISAM/VSAM index files (unless user-maintained)—for example, a customer file that requires a separate index file only because of the access method used would be counted as one file, not two, since the index would be generated and maintained by the system. However, an alphabetical index file—separate from the customer file, maintained by the application (not the system), and itself available to the user—to aid in establishing customer identity and a customer file would each be counted. As another example, if the output tape from a batch run goes back into another batch run within this same application, do *not* count it at all because it is essentially an intermediate work file which for convenience was placed on magnetic tape but provides no other user business functions other than to help process additional downstream information. If the file is a backup file, it is counted as 1 output; no other value can be ascribed this file to this application
- keys, paths, or data base segments not approved by the user
- data structures created by a COBOL "REDEFINES" statement
- other files not approved by the user.

We may now classify these files by complexity. Note from the chart on the following page that this depends on two things—the number of data items actually required by the application (not to include FILLER fields!) and either the number of record formats within the file or the number of *logical* relationships (defined as a logical association between two or more entities by way of key data in each) in which this file participates[9] to meet application requirements. This means that not all data items or relationships will be included for classification purposes. For instance, required data items are frequently attributes of the relationship rather than the entities, and therefore require a concatenated key to satisfy this requirement. The related entities may or may not be required as separate user views under the one join operation. It also means that the complexity of any given logical internal file will vary as a function of the requirements of the application using it. As we have already seen with outputs, inputs, and inquiries, no "additional factors" may be considered here with files, either. What must be considered, though, is the number of *logical relationships* in which this file participates; this is true even though the GUIDE International GPP-134 Handbook (1984) still lists only record types as the only row-entry criterion for file complexity classification. Record types

[9]For those not clear about file relationships and logical data structures, please study for a moment the below file system:

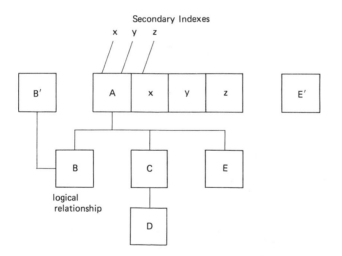

The following 16 logical data structures are represented assuming all user views are required to satisfy user requirements:

A-B, A-C-D, A-E, B′-B-A, B′-B-C-D, B′-B-E, E′, x-A-B, x-A-C-D, x-A-E, y-A-B, y-A-C-D, y-A-E, z-A-B, z-A-C-D, z-A-E.

In each case, the number of dashes (-) represents the number of relationships in the data structure and, therefore, the proper row-entry value.

belong to older, less-commonly used, design methodologies—even though several modern relational data bases support the idea of at least variable record length if not format. But this is all physical stuff—not logical. FPA can achieve maximum benefit for you *only* if implemented *correctly*, and correct implementation *demands* (it is *not* a bargaining item!) a *logical*, not physical, orientation. The key to proper file complexity determination is the *number of logical relationships in which an entity participates* and *not* the physically-oriented number of record types. That is, for each logical internal file identified, expect and look for *many* such different and unique relationships in which it participates. We are looking for *all logical* relationships, not just the one physical description. If we look only to record types and not to logical relationships, we will seriously undercount file business functions and underestimate project cost and duration. (If, however, the number of record types exceeds the number of file relationships, then use this value as the row-entry value.) This is because multiple record types are actually quite rare today, and accordingly, so would be complex files. On the other hand, many— if not most or all—files participate in multiple relationships; these files should be classified accordingly (even if they contain only a single record type) because of the additional planning, co-ordination, and integration required. Using only the record-format criterion, a single-format file can never be complex. (Not fair! "If the shoe fits, wear it!") Again, we are looking for all logical relationships, not just the one physical one.

FIGURE 6.   Files.

	1 - 19 data items referenced	20 - 50 data items referenced	51 or more data items referenced
1 logical record format/relationship	Simple (7)	Simple (7)	Average (10)
2 - 5 logical record formats/relationships	Simple (7)	Average (10)	Complex (15)
6 or more logical record formats/relationships	Average (10)	Complex (15)	Complex (15)

Do not miss *any* logical internal files! Each one missed costs you at least a whopping *24* points (7 file, 9 input, 4 output, and 4 inquiry) and very possibly much more! Missing files also costs you the use of a simple but effective estimating tool whose accuracy depends substantially on the number of files found in a system: Call each file *average* and assign to it one average output (the formatted file printout), three average inputs (the functions add, change, and delete), and one average inquiry (a quick-browse capability) for an estimated total of 32 function points per file (= 10 + 5 + 3 * 4 + 5)—then multiply the total number of *logical* internal files by this number (32) to reach a "ball park" (usually it's *low*) system size estimate. Remember that on average, files in our 13-application study contributed about 36% of the function point total; if they provide significantly less, you may have missed some—and if they provide significantly more, you may be storing information not fully utilized by the application. (Note: because, as we saw earlier, files contribute an extremely wide—from 7% to 52%—variation in contribution to final function point count, it is *not* appropriate to divide the total function point count for files by .36, even for a rough guess.)

We shall now consider the final business function group, *interfaces*—data stored elsewhere by another application but used by the one under evaluation.

INTERFACES (EI)

You should count as one interface *each* major *logical* (defined as before) file or other logical group of user-approved data or control information within the application boundary that is sent to, shared with, or received from another application. Files shared between applications are counted *both* as files *and* as interfaces within *each* application if they are actually used in both; otherwise, file credit is given only to the application actually using, maintaining, or doing work on the file (the other application would receive no file credit, but each would still receive interface credit). That is, each interface file must also be a logical internal file to this application, to some other application, or both—or it must be a transaction or print file mostly produced and assembled by the application under review. Please return to Figure 2 and note that interfaces can thus represent any of the following three situations (included classifications assume the files to be master files, not transaction; for these, the data transfer logic would be the same, but the resulting classifications would be different, as will be explained later):

1. Data or control information is passed from File A to File B. A would receive both file and interface credit, and B would receive interface credit only.
2. Data or control information is passed from File B to File A. B would receive both file and interface credit, and A would receive interface credit only.
3. Data or control information is shared between File A and File B. A and B would each receive both file and interface credit.

See the table below for a summary on how to count master file interfaces. It assumes there is a user-approved business requirement for the information imports, exports, or sharing:

file usage:	in this ("A") application, count:	in other ("B") application(s), count:
received from "B"	interface only (no updates)	both file and interface
shared with "B"	both file and interface	both file (if actually maintained) and interface
sent to "B"	both file and interface	interface only (no updates)

If you are using structured analysis and design techniques as you should be (final polite but firm reminder: "If not, *why* not? Get hot! *DO IT*!!!"), you will recall that some data or control information may be passed from within the context diagram "area under study" to an external entity (data sink, denoted by a rectangle); some data or control information may be passed from an external entity (data source, also denoted by a rectangle) to the context diagram "area under study"; and some data or control information may be shared between the external entity (still represented by a rectangle) and the context diagram "area under study." *All* such data or control information moving in one direction *to this* external entity represents one interface; *all* such data or control information moving in the opposite direction *from this* external entity represents another. If an external entity both sends data to and receives data from the context diagram "area under study," each contributing flow direction is identified and classified separately; only by coincidence will they be the same value—and only by even greater coincidence will the exact number of data items referenced be the same. After we have finished studying this one particular external entity, we would next look at all the remaining highways going to and from each of the other external entities as well, *each* direction for *each* remaining external entity representing a new and countable interface.

For example, a General Ledger application which passes account numbers to a Fixed Assets application would count one interface for *each* application, GL and FA (in addition to the file within General Ledger). This is to compensate each application for the additional design co-ordination required to ensure master file compatibility between both. Cumulative depreciation values passed by the Fixed Assets application to the General Ledger application would count as another interface (for the same reason) for *each* application, FA and GL (in addition to the file within Fixed Assets). In the first case, General Ledger would be credited with both file and interface; in the second, Fixed Assets would. In both cases, the application without file credit may still claim interface (only) credit. Interfaces are in addition to the points earned by the file standing alone, or the input/output credit (for transaction files), as appropriate.

Interfaces usually—but certainly not always—involve master files, not transaction. For FPA purposes, there is a distinct difference between logical master files and transaction files. Transactions, as we learned earlier, are events that affect or update logical internal files but together are not themselves considered logical files. Applications can interface with each other either through transactions or through logical master files. If applications interface data through transactions, then input, output, and/or inquiry credit is given—and possibly also interface. If they interface data through static master files, then interface—and perhaps also file—credit is given. The key to identifying an interface file of any kind is that an application must be able to access the data directly without the aid of another application. This is not always possible with an unprocessed transaction file, whose only order scheme is probably time and not subject or value. A transaction file (somewhat a misnomer because we remember transaction "files" are not counted as logical internal files at all, but rather instead as outputs *or* inputs, depending on which application does the work—more on this shortly) shared with another application may or may not indicate an interface, depending on whether or not conversion is required to match the record or file layout of the receiving application. For example, suppose we have a transaction file whose format is precisely the same as that required by a receiving program. In this case, we would not count any interface since no data conversion is required. Because it reached out to another application for needed data, and probably designed its data structures and definitions with this in mind, the receiving program would count one input; even though the sending program did the data-capture work, it would not count any output because it may not even know about the receiving program, and counting it as an output would be to double-count the data-transfer benefit. (There are, of course, situations in which the opposite would be true—that is, where the sending program would be credited with the output and the receiving program would be credited with nothing.) And only transaction files in which data conversion is required are candidates for interface recognition; if data conversion is not required, the transaction file is reduced in value to input or output only—and no interface credit is given either application. Now suppose the receiving application does not need to convert data because the sending application already has. In this case, the receiving application would count neither input nor interface, but the sending application would count both one output and one interface. This is to compensate the sending program for its extra work converting and redefining data into a format directly usable by the receiving program.

Sometimes, of course, the receiving application has to do its own work. When this happens—that is, when the receiving program must convert and redefine an incoming transaction file into a format it can use—it may count both one input and one interface as compensation; the sending program may count nothing.

Remember, these three situations all dealt only with transaction files, not master. For interface counting purposes, data conversion is an issue only with transaction files; even master files that do not need reformatting or redefinition are counted as interfaces (and, of course, a file)—not as input or output.

See the following table for a summary on how to count transaction or print file interfaces. It assumes there is a user-approved business requirement for these transactions to update the appropriate master file:

Transaction Files Situation:	in this ("A") application, count:		in other ("B") application(s), count:
NO DATA CONVERSION REQUIRED			
1. received from "B"	input (more common)	- or -	output
2. sent to "B"	output	- or -	input (more common)

Transaction Files Situation:	in this ("A") application, count:	in other ("B") application(s), count:
DATA CONVERSION REQUIRED		
1. received from B, A converts	both input and interface	- - - - - - -
2. received from B, B converts	- - - - - - -	both output and interface
3. sent to B, A converts	both output and interface	- - - - - - -
4. sent to B, B converts	- - - - - - -	both input and interface

Note from the table above that transaction files, unlike master, credit only one application or the other—never both. If data conversion is not an issue, the only credit provided is either input (more common) or output (less common) for one of the two applications—not both. If data conversion is an issue, the stakes are raised to "double or nothing"—one application is credited with *both* interface and *either* input *or* output, as appropriate—the other application is credited with nothing. This is not to downplay the importance of good, reliable data capture. But for FPA counting purposes, and the end-user value these rules measure, processed information is substantially more beneficial and valuable than unprocessed raw data. A cake tastes much better than any of its raw ingredients!

Look for potential interfaces from among the following:

- logical internal file accessible from another application
- logical internal file accessible to another application[10]
- shared data base[10]
- shared parameter list[10]
- exported print file
- shared transaction file requiring data conversion.

[10]These were already counted as logical internal files (although perhaps of greater complexity because not all data items will necessarily be sent to or shared with the interfacing application) but must *also* be counted as interfaces. This is because they are used by different applications for different purposes—*this* application maintains and/or modifies them in some way, making them a logical internal file; and the *other* application uses them, either as reference or to update, making them interfaces as well for each application.

Then, count as *one* interface *each* major logical (defined as before) group of user data or control information within the application that is either sent to, shared with, or received from another application:

- file of records from another application (for the other application: + 1 file, + 1 interface)
- file of records to another application (+ 1 file) (other application: + 1 interface)
- file of records to multiple applications (+ 1 file)—note that this would, however, affect the complexity weighting factor
- file of records shared between two or more applications (+ 1 file) (for the other applications: + 1 interface, + 1 file in each application actually performing maintenance as though it were its own internal file—otherwise, other applications may claim interface credit only but no file credit). For example, a file containing employee work hours generated and used by a project management application is also used by a productivity measurement application. The file is counted as one file and one interface for the productivity measurement system and as one interface and one logical internal file for the project management system because both systems take the common-format information and then do individual maintenance routines on it
- data base shared with other applications (+ 1 file)—1 interface per view *actually sent* (for the other application: + 1 file, + 1 interface per view actually received and used)
- data base shared from other applications (+ 1 file)—1 interface per view *actually received and used* (for the other application: + 1 file, + 1 interface per view)
- transaction file received from another application, data conversion required (+ 1 input). Assume a transaction tape with 22 different record formats and different logic needed to handle each format. This should be counted as 22 inputs (+ 22 interfaces if converted by this application). Now assume a transaction tape with only one record format, but that record has a transaction code field that can have 22 different values with different logic needed for each. Count this as both 22 inputs and 22 interfaces because data conversion is definitely required to translate the code field into uniquely appropriate processing logic; the code field cannot be processed directly but must instead be converted first
- transaction file sent to another application, data conversion performed (+ 1 output)
- parameter list or usercode/password list passed to or received from another application.

Note that sharing master files provides each application credit for both file and interface, but that file credit in the other two situations depends on who shipped the goods—if your ("this") application did ("sent to"), you get credit; but if the *other* application did ("received from"), *it* gets credit and you do not. For complexity sizing purposes, to be discussed shortly, count *only* those elements actually used by the receiving application (whether or not shared), not those that came along for the ride but are not actually used. This means that an interface may reference fewer data items and/or participate in fewer relationships than the parent file from which the interface came; accordingly, it also means that an interface may be less complex than the file from which it came.

However, do *not* count the following as interfaces:

- those introduced only because of the technology used (see earlier discussion under outputs)
- logical files shared between processes within the same application; in order for a logical file to be counted as an interface file, it must pass outside the application boundary (context diagram "area under study")
- logical file not required by the application but still available because physically part of another file (either internal or interface), some of which *is* needed by the application
- transaction files for which no data conversion is required; if such a file is received, an input is counted—*or* if such a file is sent, an output would be counted—the particular circumstances determine which
- message files
- other interfaces not approved by the user.

We may now classify these interfaces by complexity. Note from the following chart that this depends, as expected, on the same two things as do files—the number of data items referenced (and actually used) and the number of record formats within the file or the number of logical relationships in which the interface file participates to meet application requirements. Since an interface is exactly the same thing (although perhaps a little smaller) as a file except that it is imported into the context diagram "area under study"—not "home grown"—or that it is an entity doing business in at least two applications, the rules concerning "no additional factors" apply to interfaces as they do to files—do not use them! The same considerations about record types and formats apply here, too, of course—in precisely the same way as with our discussion on files. As there, the key to proper interface identification is the *number of logical relationships in which an entity participates* and *not* the physically-oriented number of record types. Use of the structured analysis and design technique described earlier will help you easily find all existing interfaces; we are looking here again for *all* these *logical* relationships, not the one physical description. Expect and look for many such logical relationships and rate the interface complexity accordingly, just as we did for files.

FIGURE 7. Interfaces.

	1 - 19 data items referenced	20 - 50 data items referenced	51 or more data items referenced
1 logical record format/relationship	Simple (5)	Simple (5)	Average (7)
2 - 5 logical record formats/relationships	Simple (5)	Average (7)	Complex (10)
6 or more logical record formats/relationships	Average (7)	Complex (10)	Complex (10)

Do not miss *any* external interfaces! They usually provide 5 or 7 points each, although many applications do not require them.

Whew! We have now completed step one, the identification and classification of function point business functions for each major application group—outputs, inquiries, inputs, files, and interfaces. For each, the process was essentially the same. We identified what was, and was not, a valid business function, then determined how difficult this benefit was to provide as a measure of eventual end-user value. This procedure, and the resulting measure of value, are *exactly the same* for all 250 computer languages in which your system may be written—no exceptions! We saw the importance of clear and logical thinking and attention to detail; imprecise thinking or carelessness may force you to sell the farm! Multiple errors in either classification—but especially in identification—can cause you great pain and grief, discomfort that can easily be prevented by proper training and due care. DON'T OVERLOOK ANYTHING! And if you are in doubt about how to classify a benefit and additional detail is not possible or readily available, call it average. You will not be turned away from Heaven's Gates if it is otherwise!

*** IT IS MORE IMPORTANT TO IDENTIFY A BUSINESS FUNCTION THAN TO CLASSIFY IT! ***

Before we go on to step two—adjusting the total function point count just determined according to various production environment factors—we need to practice identifying, classifying, and posting business functions to the appropriate forms. For your convenience, a quick-reference summary table is provided on the next page.

FIGURE 8.   Quick-Reference Summary Table.

OUTPUT:
DATA ITEMS

FILES		1 - 5	6 - 19	20+
	<2	S (4)	S (4)	A (5)
	2 - 3	S (4)	A (5)	C (7)
	>3	A (5)	C (7)	C (7)

INPUT:
DATA ITEMS

FILES		1 - 4	5 - 15	16+
	<2	S (3)	S (3)	A (4)
	2	S (3)	A (4)	C (6)
	>2	A (4)	C (6)	C (6)

INQUIRIES:
SELECT THE GREATER OF INPUT OR OUTPUT PART

FILES AND INTERFACES:
DATA ITEMS

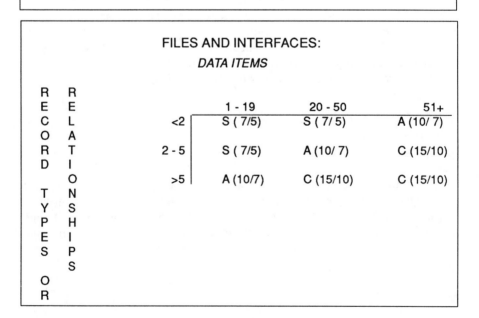

RECORD TYPES OR	RELATIONSHIPS		1 - 19	20 - 50	51+
		<2	S (7/5)	S (7/ 5)	A (10/ 7)
		2 - 5	S (7/5)	A (10/ 7)	C (15/10)
		>5	A (10/7)	C (15/10)	C (15/10)

2

On-line Parts System FPA Example

As mentioned previously, the purpose of this exercise is to practice identifying, classifying, and posting business functions in a small but realistic system. Assume we already have in production a batch parts inventory system. We now wish to add to this system the following on-line, menu-driven capabilities:

- on-line request for reports
- on-line display of parts inventory
- on-line display of parts description
- on-line file maintenance.

Due to various storage, performance, and response time constraints, the entire Parts Master File will not be used in the new on-line system. (It will, of course, continue to be used in the existing batch system.) Instead, only a portion of it will be contained in the Selected-Parts File. The parts in this file will all be selected from the Parts Master File and will usually be those in highest demand. Users will be able to identify Master File parts they wish added to the Selected-Parts File. Similarly, they will also be able to identify Selected-Parts File parts they no longer wish contained in that file. Both will be done through a Parts Selection Table, which will relate items in the Selected-Parts File to those in the master and maintain a current record count of the former.

A control report should be provided to list all recent changes to the Selected-Parts File and report its current (defined as the end of the previous business day) size and status. A printed Parts Inventory Report should also be provided; this report will be requested by terminal operators and will list parts contained in the Selected-Parts File.

In addition to the Parts Master File, which is an external entity and thus will not be used directly, note that system design and performance considerations indicate two more physical files will be required. One of these is the Parts Selection Table; it consists only of the data items part-number and size-code and logically relates only to the Parts Master File (through the batch interface). The other physical file is the Selected-Parts File. It is formatted precisely the same as the master file and consists of two logical files, the Parts Description File and the Parts Location File, each of which logically relates only to the Parts Master File (also through the batch interface). The Parts Description logical file consists of the following data items:

- part-number
- size-code
- description
- unit-price
- remarks.

The key to this logical file is the data items together part-number, size-code, and description.

The Parts Location logical file consists of the following data items:

- part-number
- size-code
- location-ID
- stock-available
- stock-on-order
- date-ordered.

The key to this logical file is the data items together part-number, size-code, and location-ID.

It may help you now to draw a brief but complete system flowchart. (Note: for more complex applications than this, I would also draw a leveled-and-balanced data flow diagram network. But since the system flowchart effectively displays all the various major business functions of an application *well before* individual data structures and items are named and organized, a

system flowchart is the more effective tool when only the requirements definition report is available. In *this* system, of course, we are finishing the design
phase and are well past the requirements definition 5% milestone!) As you do
this, be sure you include all user business functions and think about how they
will be classified. When you are done, compare your sketch with one possible
solution presented below:

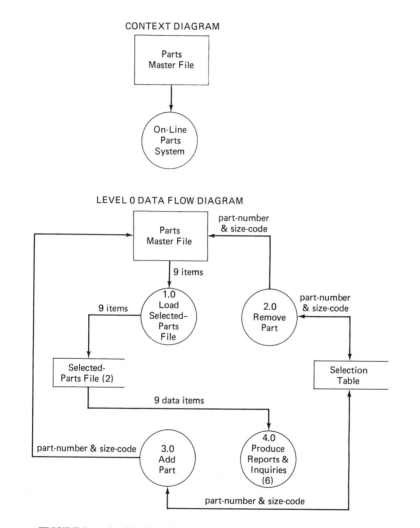

FIGURE 9A.   On-Line Parts System Context and Level 0 Data Flow Diagram.

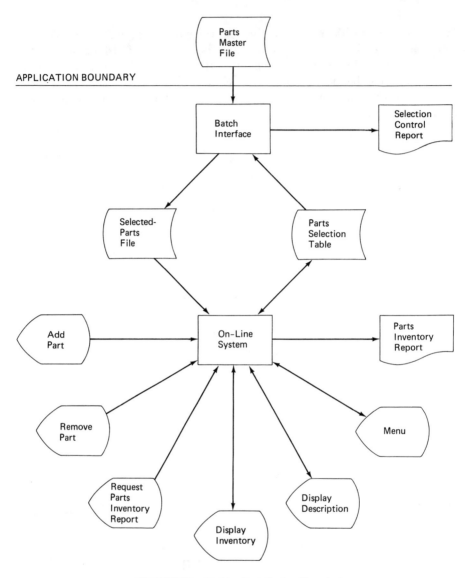

FIGURE 9B. On-Line Parts System Flowchart.

If you did not include all these business functions, please reread the system description and find out why. None of these business functions can be omitted. Now that they have been identified, let's classify them. Since this is a new system, outputs, inquiries, and inputs should be classified before files and interfaces. (In Chapter 5 we shall learn that the proper evaluation order for an *existing* system undergoing maintenance or enhancement is files and interfaces *first*, then outputs, inquiries, and inputs—more on this in Chapter 5.) Study carefully the sample screens and reports provided on the next several pages, reviewing as necessary the rules given earlier. For each business function group (function type), be sure to list all business functions identified and classified, complete with reasons why you classified them the way you did— that is, how many files or relationships (row values) you entered and how many data items (column values) you entered in the classification process. Remember, it is more important to identify a business function than to classify it—but for so small a system as this (and completely designed, too), we really should not miss the mark on either count. You may wish to copy a blank Detail Sheet from the back of this book for each of the five business function groups, and a Summary Sheet on which to post the totals. Work carefully and review the rules presented in Chapter 1 as necessary. GOOD LUCK!

```
+------------------------------------------------------------------------+
|                          ON-LINE PARTS SYSTEM                          |
|                         PARTS INVENTORY REPORT                         |
|                                                                        |
|                                                         Page: 999      |
|                                                                        |
|   DATE:          MM/DD/YY                                              |
|   TIME:          HH:MM:SS                                              |
|                                                                        |
|   PART #         XXXXXXXXXX                                            |
|   SIZE CODE      XXXXXX                                                |
|   DESCRIPTION    XXXXXXXXXXXXXXXXXXXXXXXXXXXXXXXXXX                     |
|   UNIT PRICE     99,999.99                                             |
|                                                                        |
|      LOCATION      AVAILABLE        ON ORDER       DATE ORDERED         |
|      XXXXXX        9,999,999        9,999,999      MM/DD/YY             |
|      XXXXXX        9,999,999        9,999,999      MM/DD/YY             |
|      XXXXXX        9,999,999        9,999,999      MM/DD/YY             |
|       TOTAL       99,999,999       99,999,999                          |
+------------------------------------------------------------------------+
```

ON-LINE PARTS SYSTEM

SELECTION CONTROL REPORT

Page: 999

DATE: MM/DD/YY

TIME: HH:MM:SS

PARTS ADDED

PART #	SIZE CODE	DESCRIPTION
XXXXXXXXXX	XXXXX	XXXXXXXXXXXXXXXXXXXXXXXXXXXXXXXX
XXXXXXXXXX	XXXXX	XXXXXXXXXXXXXXXXXXXXXXXXXXXXXXXX

PARTS REMOVED

PART #	SIZE CODE	DESCRIPTION
XXXXXXXXXX	XXXXX	XXXXXXXXXXXXXXXXXXXXXXXXXXXXXXXX
XXXXXXXXXX	XXXXX	XXXXXXXXXXXXXXXXXXXXXXXXXXXXXXXX

INVALID REQUESTS

PART #	SIZE CODE	REASON
XXXXXXXXXX	XXXXX	XXXXXXXXXXXXXXXXXXXXXXXXXXXXXXXX

SUMMARY

Page: 999

SELECTED-PARTS FILE CONTAINED   99,999,999   PARTS BEFORE THIS RUN

99,999 PARTS ADDED

99,999 PARTS REMOVED

SELECTED-PARTS FILE NOW CONTAINS   99,999,999 PARTS

NET CHANGE   999,999 PARTS

```
ON-LINE PARTS SYSTEM


THE FOLLOWING FUNCTIONS ARE AVAILABLE:

    1  DISPLAY PART DESCRIPTION

    2  DISPLAY PART INVENTORY (ONE LOCATION)

    3  PRINT PART INVENTORY (ALL LOCATIONS)

    4  ADD NEW PART TO SELECTION TABLE

    5  REMOVE PART FROM SELECTION TABLE

    6  EXIT

YOUR SELECTION: ▶_◀
```

Error messages: Invalid function
                   Function not available

```
ON-LINE PARTS SYSTEM


DISPLAY PART DESCRIPTION

PLEASE ENTER:   PART # ▶................◀

                SIZE CODE ▶............◀

DESCRIPTION:    XXXXXXXXXXXXXXXXXXXXXXXXXXXXXXX

SIZE:           XXXXXXXXXXXXXXX

UNIT PRICE:     99,999.99

REMARKS:        XXXXXXXXXXXXXXXXXXXXXXXXXXXXXXX
                XXXXXXXXXXXXXXXXXXXXXXXXXXXXXXX
```

Error messages: Invalid part # or size code
                   Part not found on file

```
ON-LINE PARTS SYSTEM

DISPLAY PART INVENTORY

PLEASE ENTER:   PART # ▶...............◀

                SIZE CODE ▶...........◀

                LOCATION ID ▶........◀

DESCRIPTION:    XXXXXXXXXXXXXXXXXXXXXXXXXXXXXXX
LOCATION:       XXXXXXXXXXXXXXXXXXXXXXXXXXXXXXX
AVAILABLE:      9,999,999
ON ORDER:       9,999,999
        NEXT LOCATION? (Y/N) ▶__◀
```

Invalid part #, size code, or location ID
Part or location not found

```
ON-LINE PARTS SYSTEM


ADD NEW PART TO SELECTION TABLE

PLEASE ENTER:   PART # ▶..............◀

                SIZE CODE ▶..........◀

***NOTE THAT DETAILS FOR THIS PART WILL BE
AVAILABLE ON THE NEXT BUSINESS DAY***
```

Error messages: Invalid part # or size code
                  Part already on file

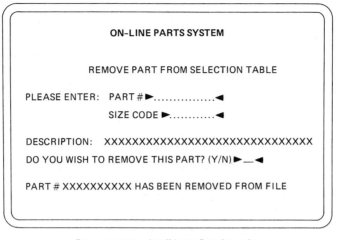

ON-LINE PARTS SYSTEM

REMOVE PART FROM SELECTION TABLE

PLEASE ENTER: PART # ▶...............◀

                SIZE CODE ▶...........◀

DESCRIPTION: XXXXXXXXXXXXXXXXXXXXXXXXXXXXXX

DO YOU WISH TO REMOVE THIS PART? (Y/N) ▶__◀

PART # XXXXXXXXXX HAS BEEN REMOVED FROM FILE

Error messages: Invalid part # or size code
                  Part not on file

ON-LINE PARTS SYSTEM

PRINT PART INVENTORY

PLEASE ENTER: PART # ▶...............◀

                SIZE CODE ▶...........◀

REPORT SENT TO PRINT QUEUE

Erro messages: Invalid part # or size code
                 Part not on file
                 Print queue closed

How many did you find—70? Super! Let's see how we got—or why we did not get—this figure. First, look at the outputs, beginning with the Parts Inventory Report. Note that six data items are listed in the header portion of the report and four data items are listed in the detail portion. Also note the totals line. Date and time are provided by the system. Part-number and size-code are provided by both the Parts Description File and the Parts Location File. The next two data items, description and unit-price, are provided only by the Parts Description File. The remaining four are provided by the Parts Location File. To produce the Parts Inventory Report, then, requires access to two logical files (plus the system clock, but this does not matter). From Figure 8 we see that ten data items referenced from two logical files represents an average output.

But we are not yet done with this report. Recall that an output is considered unique if it has a different format or requires different processing logic. Now look at the totals line of the Parts Inventory Report. Even though both data items, total-stock-available and total-stock-on-order, are lined up underneath their corresponding detail items, the format for this line is different from that of the detail lines. This is not just because the word "TOTAL" replaces the part location and blanks replace the order date in the detail line. More significantly, this total line would be considered a separate output because different processing logic is required to total the data items stock-available and stock-on-order than simply to list them. Neither is the end-user value of this totals line open to question, especially if many warehouses or bins are involved. Do not discount a report's importance because it contains but a few data items! This totals line must be considered a separate report. (IFPUG dissents.) It requires access to only one logical file, the Parts Location File, and reports only two data items. From Figure 8 we see that two data items referenced from one logical file represents a simple output.

Note that the Selection Control Report consists of two parts, a detail report and a summary report. The detail report lists six data items—date and time from the system; part-number and size-code from the Parts Selection Table (whose purpose is to accumulate parts by number and by size added to, or removed from, the Selected-Parts File); description from the Parts Description File; and reason from a user-maintained error message table. To produce the six-item Selection Control Detail Report, then, requires access to three logical files—the Parts Selection Table, the Description File, and the Error Message Table. From Figure 8 we see that six data items referenced from three logical files also represents an average output.

The Selection Control Summary Report lists five data items—file size before the run, number of parts added, number of parts removed, current file size, and the net change value, which is calculated and printed but not stored. The number of parts added and removed is provided by the Parts Selection Table, and previous and current file sizes are provided by the Selected-Parts File. In this case, it does not matter which logical file actually provides the count; the result would be the same for either. To produce the five-item Selection Control Summary Report, then, requires access to two logical files—the Selection Table and either logical file of the Selected-Parts File. From Figure 8 we see that five data items referenced from two logical files represents a simple output.

These four reports—the Parts Inventory Detail and Totals Reports, the Selection Control Detail Report, and the Selection Control Summary Report—are all the output the new on-line system will provide. Both detail reports are average; both summary reports are simple. They would be listed on the Detail Sheet as shown in Figure 10.

FIGURE 10.   On-Line Parts Outputs—Detail.

Detail Sheet

Application: On-line Parts				Function Type: Outputs	
Description:			Simple	Average	Complex
Parts Inventory Report - 2 reports					
1. Detail report (2 files, 10 data items)				1	
2. Summary report (1 file, 2 data items)			1		
Selection Control Report - 2 reports					
1. Detail report (3 files, 6 data items)				1	
2. Summary report (2 files, 5 data items)			1		
		*** TOTALS ***	2	2	

They would be totalled on the Summary Sheet like this:

FIGURE 11.   On-Line Parts Outputs—Summary.

Business Function	Application: On-line Parts					
	Number	Complexity		Factor	Line Total	Group Total
OUTPUTS	2	Simple	*	4	=	8	
	2	Average	*	5	=	10	
	0	Complex	*	7	=	0	
TOTAL:	4					18

Now let's look at what inquiries this system will provide. The first one is extremely easy. The Main Menu passes only one data item—the function selection number—to the system, accesses no files, and literally is simple as possible.

The next inquiry, the Parts Description Display ("DISPLAY PART DESCRIPTION"), consists of an input portion and an output portion both on the same screen. The input portion requests two data items, namely part-number and size-code. Both of these are found in the Parts Description File. They are also found in the Parts Location File, but we know this will not be the file searched; one benefit of the menu we just listed is that it narrows the search for information and then improves response time. So the input portion of this inquiry is simple. The output portion of this inquiry lists four data items—description, size, unit-price, and remarks. All of these may be found in the Parts Description File. The output for this inquiry, like the input, is simple. So is the inquiry.

The last inquiry, the Parts Inventory Display ("DISPLAY PART INVEN-TORY"), also consists of a single dual-function screen. To the input portion is now added the data item location-ID. All of these are found in the Parts Location File. Unless three or more files are accessed, which does not happen here, three data items referenced indicate a simple input portion. The output portion of this inquiry also consists of three data items from this file—location, stock-available, and stock-on-order—but also brings along description from the Parts Description File. Although two logical files are accessed, the output is still simple, as is the inquiry.

These three inquiries—the Main Menu, the Parts Description Display, and the Parts Inventory Display—are all the inquiries the new on-line system will provide. All simple, they would be listed on the Detail Sheet as shown in Figure 12.

FIGURE 12.   On-Line Parts Inquiries—Detail.

Detail Sheet			
Application: On-line Parts	Function Type: Inquiries		
Description:	Simple	Average	Complex
Main Menu (0 files, 1 data item)	1		
Parts Description Display (1 file, 4 data items output)	1		
Parts Inventory Display (2 files, 4 data items output)	1		
*** TOTALS ***	3		

They would be totalled on the Summary Sheet like this:

FIGURE 13.   On-Line Parts Inquiries—Summary.

Business Function	Application: On-line Parts					
	Number	Complexity		Factor	Line Total	Group Total
INQUIRIES	3	Simple	*	4 =	12	
	0	Average	*	5 =	0	
	0	Complex	*	6 =	0	
	0	Complex	*	7 =	0	
TOTAL:	3					12

We shall now consider inputs. Recall from the requirements definition and system flowchart there will be three inputs into this system. They are:

1. to add a part to the Parts Selection Table
2. to remove a part from the Parts Selection Table, and
3. to request the Parts Inventory Report.

Note that adding a part to the Parts Selection Table requires the operator to enter two data items, part-number and size-code. Only the Parts Selection Table is accessed during this transaction, so from Figure 8 we determine this function to be simple.

Now look at the Remove-Part screen. This screen also requires the operator to enter part-number and size-code. When he or she does, a description of the part entered appears on the bottom half of the screen along with a confirmation message to which the operator must respond; this confirmation response counts as one data item for complexity classification purposes. The description, as we have already seen, is provided by the Parts Description File. For this transaction, two files are accessed—the Parts Selection Table (for part-number and size-code) and the Parts Description File (for description). With only four data items (remember to include the operator response as one data item), though, the function remains simple.

(Note: Even though this operation may appear similar to an inquiry, it clearly is not. The reason the part description is displayed is to show the operator he or she made the right choice of part before it is removed from the Selected-Parts File. Since the purpose of the transaction as a whole is to update the Selected-Parts File by deleting a record no longer wanted, this transaction can only be an input because inquiries never update files. Neither is it a "tell me what's in the data base..." combination of inquiry and input because in this transaction I already know what's there and what I want to do with it; the only thing I really need is confirmation of my entry. In an inquiry-followed-by-update combined operation, I don't know what's there—so want to browse—and don't know what, if anything, to change—or how to change it! We shall see in the next chapter that confirmation messages such as this are also accounted for in the Adjustment Factor calculations.)

Finally, look at the Parts Inventory Report request screen. Its purpose is to allow the user to select desired parts and sizes to be printed on the Parts Inventory Report we studied earlier as an output. Required entries for this screen are also part-number and size-code, both from the Parts Selection Table. (This screen looks very similar to the add-part screen just studied; because of clearly different logic, though, it represents a separate business function.) This function is also simple.

These three inputs—adding a part to the Parts Selection Table, removing a part from it, and requesting a Parts Inventory Report printout—are all the inputs needed by the new on-line system. All simple, they would be listed on the Detail Sheet as shown in Figure 14.

FIGURE 14.   On-Line Parts Inputs—Detail.

Detail Sheet			
Application: On-line Parts	Function Type: Inputs		
Description:	Simple	Average	Complex
Add part to Selection Table (1 file, 2 data items)	1		
Remove part from Selection Table (2 files, 4 data items)	1		
Request Parts Inventory Report (1 file, 2 data items)	1		
*** TOTALS ***	3		

They would be totalled on the Summary Sheet like this:

FIGURE 15.   On-Line Parts Inputs—Summary.

Business Function	Application: On-line Parts							
	Number	Complexity		Factor		Line Total	Group Total
INPUTS	3	Simple	*	3	=	9	
	0	Average	*	4	=	0	
	0	Complex	*	6	=	0	
TOTAL:	3						9

From the requirements definition report and accompanying design specifications, we have already done most of the work classifying this system's files. Recall the Parts Selection Table consists of two data items, part-number and size-code, participating in but a single relationship (with Parts Master File). This file would be classified as simple. The other physical file is the Selected-Parts File. Since this file has two keys—consisting of the data items part-number, size-code, and either description or location-ID—it consists of two logical files. These logical files are referred to as the Parts Description File and the Parts Location File, after the third and determining key item. Both logical files participate in but a single relationship (with Parts Master File); the former contains five data items, and the latter contains six. Like the Parts Selection Table, these two files would each be classified simple and listed on the Detail Sheet as shown in Figure 16.

FIGURE 16.   On-Line Parts Files—Detail.

Detail Sheet

Application: On-line Parts			
		Function Type: Files	
Description:	Simple	Average	Complex
Parts Selection Table (1 relationship, 2 data items)	1		
Selected-Parts File - 2 logical files			
1. Parts Description (1 relationship, 5 data items)	1		
2. Parts Location (1 relationship, 6 data items)	1		
*** TOTALS ***	3		

They would be totalled on the Summary Sheet as follows:

FIGURE 17.   On-Line Parts Files—Summary.

Business Function	Application: On-line Parts						
	Number	Complexity		Factor		Line Total	Group Total
FILES	3	Simple	*	7	=	21	
	0	Average	*	10	=	0	
	0	Complex	*	15	=	0	
TOTAL:	3						21

Finally, we consider the interfaces present in this system. Recall from the requirements definition report and the system flowchart that this program relates parts in the Parts Selection Table to the Parts Master File. Since neither of these files is a transaction file, the question of data conversion does not arise. Because the Selected-Parts File is formatted precisely the same as is the Parts Master File, participates in only this relationship, and uses all data items from the Parts Master File, we need to count one interface for each of the two logical files. These interfaces would be listed on the Detail Sheet as shown in Figure 18.

FIGURE 18.   On-Line Parts Interfaces—Detail.

Detail Sheet

Application: On-line Parts			
		Function Type: Interfaces	
Description:	Simple	Average	Complex
Parts Master File to Selected-Parts File - 2 logical files			
1. Parts Description (1 relationship, 5 data items)	1		
2. Parts Location (1 relationship, 6 data items)	1		
*** TOTALS ***	2		

They would be totalled like this on the Summary Sheet:

FIGURE 19.   On-Line Parts Interfaces—Summary.

Business Function	Number	Complexity		Factor		Line Total	Group Total
		Application: On-line Parts					
INTERFACES	2	Simple	*	5	=	10	
	0	Average	*	7	=	0	
	0	Complex	*	10	=	0	
TOTAL:	2						10

Combining all the business function groups would give us the following:

FIGURE 20.   On-Line Parts: Total System Summary.

Business Function	Number	Complexity		Factor		Line Total	Group Total
		Application: On-line Parts					
OUTPUTS	2	Simple	*	4	=	8	
	2	Average	*	5	=	10	
	0	Complex	*	7	=	0	
TOTAL:	4						18
INQUIRIES	3	Simple	*	4	=	12	
	0	Average	*	5	=	0	
	0	Complex	*	6	=	0	
	0	Complex	*	7	=	0	
TOTAL:	3						12
INPUTS	3	Simple	*	3	=	9	
	0	Average	*	4	=	0	
	0	Complex	*	6	=	0	
TOTAL:	3						9
FILES	3	Simple	*	7	=	21	
	0	Average	*	10	=	0	
	0	Complex	*	15	=	0	
TOTAL:	3						21
INTERFACES	2	Simple	*	5	=	10	
	0	Average	*	7	=	0	
	0	Complex	*	10	=	0	
TOTAL:	2						10
TOTAL UNADJUSTED FUNCTION POINTS:							70

Relating these values to the system flowchart drawn earlier, we would have:

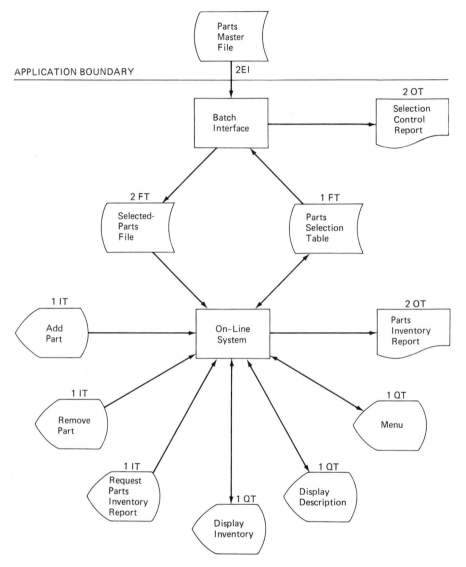

FIGURE 21.   On-Line Parts System Flowchart with Function Points Identified.

Feeling confident now? Want to try something a little more challenging? If so, then following are three screens—

Sales Analysis with Summarized Totals	(Report)
Sales Analysis with Print Totals Only	(Report)
Product Inquiry	(Inquiry)

from R & D Systems' quality general-accounting software package, "GAP."
All information provided on the two Sales Analysis reports is stored in and
maintained by the INSALES master file with the exception of the data items
customer-name, sales-YTD, cost-YTD, gross-margin, and per-cent-margin.
These data items are all stored in and maintained by the accounts receivable
master file ARMAST.

SALES ANALYSIS WITH SUMMARIZED TOTALS:

```
--------------------------------------------------------------------------
DATE 05-15-84  THRU  08-23-84     DAY THUR      TIME 18:49    OP: DOC   PAGE   1
                             R&D DEMO-COMPANY #1
                       S A L E S   A N A L Y S I S   R E P O R T
                      SALES BY CUSTOMER BY PRODUCT CATEGORY

CUST #     CUSTOMER NAME        SALES YTD    COST YTD    GROSS MARGIN        %MARGIN
STOCK NO          P CAT     UNITS   NET SALES  DISCOUNT          COST
DESCRIPTION                 INVOICE #
------------------------------------------------------------------------------------
    1 A-1 SYSTEMS INC.                  .00        .00             .00            .00
                            444444
                            111111
                            555555
                            333333
                            222222
                               520
                               521
* CATEGORY TOTAL    0       7.00    21589.84       .00             .00         100.00
------------------------------------------------------------------------------------

                              1000
                              1000
* CATEGORY TOTAL    1        .00      140.00       .00           90.00          35.71
------------------------------------------------------------------------------------

                            111112
                              4300
                              4220
                               540
                                70
                                63
                            111130
                            111139
* CATEGORY TOTAL  110      36.00     8255.77    422.98         3932.73          52.36
------------------------------------------------------------------------------------

                            111111
                                 0
* CATEGORY TOTAL  120      24.00     3225.60    134.40         1920.00          40.47
------------------------------------------------------------------------------------

                                 0
                                 0
                                70
                                63
                            111139
                                 0
                                 0
* CATEGORY TOTAL  130      11.00    45855.07   4317.46        27230.00          40.61
------------------------------------------------------------------------------------
```

```
                                78
                                78
                                79
                            111111
                               134
* CATEGORY TOTAL   140     45.00          99.40          12.60          62.25          37.37
---------------------------------------------------------------------------------

* CUSTOMER TOTAL     1    123.00       79165.68        4887.44       45930.70          58.02
```

SALES ANALYSIS WITH PRINT TOTALS ONLY:

```
---------------------------------------------------------------------------------
DATE 05-15-84  THRU  08-23-84     DAY THUR       TIME 18:49    OP: DOC    PAGE   1
                                R&D DEMO-COMPANY #1
                        S A L E S   A N A L Y S I S   R E P O R T
                        SALES BY CUSTOMER BY PRODUCT CATEGORY
```

CUST#	CUSTOMER NAME		SALES YTD	COST YTD	GROSS MARGIN		%MARGIN
STOCK NO		P CAT	UNITS	NET SALES	DISCOUNT	COST	
DESCRIPTION			INVOICE#				

```
---------------------------------------------------------------------------------
    1 A-1 SYSTEMS INC                    .00           .00                    .00           .00
* CUSTOMER TOTAL     1    123.00       79165.68     4887.44       45930.70          58.02

    2 ABOTT BUS. SUPP      39963.58       23123.37              16840.21          42.14
* CUSTOMER TOTAL     2     90.00     44136.58       4633.27       18613.21          42.17

    3 ADOM ELECTRONIC     328292.28     249022.46              80689.55          24.47
* CUSTOMER TOTAL     3   1089.00    326878.18  102375.68       78989.32          24.16

    4 ADVANCED SYSTEM     103655.01      50565.38              53289.63          51.31
* CUSTOMER TOTAL     4    488.00    101567.51     6089.95       52412.13          51.60

    5 AGRI-TIRE SUPPL     116224.65      80012.85              77000.70          49.04
* CUSTOMER TOTAL     5    569.00    111076.05     7789.40       34321.30          30.90

*** GRAND TOTALS ***    2359.00    662824.00  125775.74       230266.66          34.74
```

We first need to sort out how many different reports are presented. Unless the summarized-totals sales analysis report covers only one customer, the answer to this question is "four reports": the detail report, the Category Total report, the Customer Total report, and (not shown, but assumed) the Grand Totals report.

All four of these reports access both files mentioned. The detail report is complex because it displays 20 data items (some of which may be calculated items). The remaining three reports each display six, so are each average.

For the other Sales Analysis report, we first see that three individual reports are included: the detail report, the Customer Total report, and the Grand Totals report. The column headers are the same as we just saw, but not all are used in this report. However, the same two files as before are accessed for each report. The detail report displays 12 data items and is average; the Customer Total report displays six data items and is also average; and the Grand Totals report, falling short by one data item (product-category), drops to simple.

PRODUCT INQUIRY

```
     DATE    DAY      COMPANY NAME       TIME    VERSION #    INITIALS
  ================== INVENTORY CONTROL / I N Q U I R Y ==================
 |STOCK NO. .            |PRODUCT CATEGORY ..  |SALES YTD ...$
 |DESC                   |UNITS .      LOC ..  |RETURNS YTD .$
 |AVERAGE COST .....     |PRICE PER ........   |COST YTD ....$
 |REPLACEMENT COST .     |ON HAND              |ISSUES YTD ...
 |STANDARD COST ....     |RESERVED             |SALES LAST YR $
 |TAX   COMM%            |ON ORDER             |ISSUES LAST YR ..
 |SUB STOCK#             |RECEIVED             |  PRICES    DISCOUNTS
 |LAST SALE DATE ......  |NET AVAIL            |  1              1
 |LAST RECEIPT DATE ...  |QTY BRK 1 ........   |  2              2
 |PRICE         DISCOUNT |QTY BRK 2 ........   |  3              3
 |BASE PRICE ......      |QTY BRK 3 ........   |  4              4
 |--------------------------------------------------------------------
 |
 |
 |
 |
 |
 |
 |
 |
 |STOCK# [            ]           PRINT?  [N]
 |WHSE# [  ] UNITS [    ] START [      ] PRINTER [    ] SHORT NAME [      ]
  ====================================================================
```

<u>DESCRIPTION</u>

This screen is used to enter parameters and to display Inventory
Control Inquiries. Three Inquiry formats can be accessed from
this screen.

- <u>Product Inquiry</u>: The product information from ICMAST and the
  data stored in ICWHSE for that product are displayed.

- <u>Warehouse Inquiry</u>: The product information from ICMAST and
  the transactions from ICHIST for that product and warehouse
  are displayed.

- <u>Product Name Inquiry</u>: A list of the products which exist in
  ICMAST are displayed.

Now let's look for a moment at the Product Inquiry screen. Note from the
description below it that this screen actually constitutes three inquiries of the same
format but different processing logic. In each case, all information provided above
the dotted line is stored in and maintained by the inventory control master file IC-
MAST. Information below the dotted line is stored in and maintained by the in-

ventory control warehouse file ICWHSE, or by the inventory control history file ICHIST.

Depending on intended use, this inquiry may be either simple (Product Name Inquiry) or complex (Product/Warehouse Inquiry). In all three cases, it is the output portion which determines this. For Product Inquiry, did you find 46 output data items in two files? I hope so! Product Inquiry, then, is complex. For Warehouse Inquiry, did you find 51 output data items in two files? You should have found the same 46 items you found in Product Inquiry; these numbers already guarantee that Warehouse Inquiry is also complex. But as things turn out, five additional data items (transaction-type, reference-number, transaction-units, transaction-date, and transaction-cost/sale) are also displayed in the lower portion of the screen. Finally, Product Name Inquiry is simple; it lists only elementary information (name, stock-number, and product category) from a single file. See how well you're doing now? Keep up the good work!

3

FPA General Application Characteristics: Rules and On-line Parts System Example

In the previous two chapters, we learned how to identify and count function points. We were concerned with the "*what*" of things—that is, with the *logical* system. In this chapter, we recognize that "one size does *not* fit all." This means the same *logical* system will vary in actual implementation according to the "*how*" of things—the objectives and the hardware/software configuration of the particular shop environment in which the logical system is installed. Although Function Point Analysis is rightfully oriented toward the logical, not physical, view of systems, it fully and also correctly recognizes that the specific shop environment can and does play an important role in how a given system is implemented. This treatment of the physical environmental influences is provided by the 14 adjustment factors we shall study shortly. As we do, keep these two points clearly in mind:

1. The unadjusted function point count (what we did in Chapters 1 and 2) is the *logical* system and therefore *always* remains *exactly the same* regardless of where it is implemented and the language in which it is written—no exceptions!

2. The 14 adjustment factors we shall soon learn represent applicable elements of the *physical* system, vary (except by coincidence) from one shop to another, and adjust the value of the logical system accordingly.

Adjusting function points is even easier to do than identifying them. Here we shall adjust the raw total just calculated according to the contribution—*as seen by the users*—by each of the following production environment factors which influence the system as a whole and not just a particular function:

1. data communications
2. distributed data or processing
3. performance objectives
4. heavily-used configuration
5. transaction rate
6. on-line data entry
7. end user efficiency
8. on-line update
9. complex processing
10. reusability
11. conversion and installation ease
12. operational ease
13. multiple-site use
14. facilitate change.

Collectively, these are known as the General Application Characteristics—or "Processing Complexity" in earlier works.

Definitions for each of these factors will be given shortly. As was the case with functions, count and fairly evaluate only those factors which clearly benefit the end user, factors to which the end user agrees. Do not count factors necessary to support technical requirements of the production environment or the coding language, or those you used as an excuse to fill your toybox with all the "latest and greatest" toys! Count only those factors which:

- are specifically approved by the user (note, however, a user may still approve a factor only indirectly specified or implied in the requirements definition report; the factor, so long as specifically approved, need not be specifically stated); again, don't take a "free ride" to fill your wish list (ask Santa Claus to do that, not your users!)—and
- influence to a measurable degree the design, development, implementation, or support of an application.

With these considerations in mind, let us now define each of these factors (General Application Characteristics) more precisely:

1. *Data communications* means that data or control information used in the application is sent or received over data communication facilities—including not only various networks, concentrators, multiplexers, and private lines, but also the terminals locally connected. On-line systems, therefore, will always have at least some data communications influence.

2. *Distributed data or processing* indicates the application uses data stored, accessed, or processed on a storage or processing system other than the one used in the main program routines. Note that presence of this factor increases the data communications influence previously defined.

3. *Application performance objectives* influence system design, development, implementation, and support when specific, user-approved demands for exceptionally high throughput or fast response times have been made.

4. If the application will be run in a *heavily used, tight, or crowded configuration*, extra design and programming care is required to minimize storage access routines and swapping code segments in and out of main memory. This factor would be especially important to a user already lacking computer capacity but unable to purchase or acquire more hardware or upgraded software; the system is "running out of gas."

5. *A high transaction rate* can occur when the network consists of many data entry or inquiry terminals, when each screen transmitted contains a lot of input information, or when the frequency of screen transmission is high. Greater design efficiency is required due to the increased competition for line and central processor facilities.

6. *On-line inquiry and data entry* (including control and security functions) are always more difficult to accommodate than similar batch systems; hardware, application software, and operating system software are all affected by the additional requirements of an on-line system.

7. When *end user efficiency* is emphasized, more human-factor features are required; these are designed to increase the level of "user-friendliness" and include such things as conversational data entry (requiring multiple sequenced screens), help screens, "next format" fields, paging capabilities, more descriptive documentation (including users manuals and "learner-friendly" training materials), second-language input/output screens and messages, and additional edit, error trap, and exception handling routines. If you are using structured systems analysis and design techniques, the boundary of the physical system—the "human-machine interface"—is high.

8. As are on-line inquiry and data entry more difficult than batch, so is *on-line update* of files and data sets more difficult because of the short turnaround time and its widespread effects on all system design components. On-line update requires non-sequential disk files and reliable transaction files for both production and audit/recovery purposes.

9. *Complex processing* refers to the situation in which an application requires substantially greater than average difficulty in input or output processing; in logic, file, or numeric manipulation; or in exception handling routines. For example, an application requiring multiple control interactions and decision points would be classified as complex. So would one requiring extensive logical or mathematical equations, such as forecasting future sales using multiple forecasting models. As a third example, an application which sorts out many transactions for correction and reprocessing ("rework") would also be considered complex. Finally, processing requiring high security measures or sensitive controls would be accounted for here.

10. *Code reusability* refers to the situation in which some of an application's routines, subroutines, or other procedures have been designed or written with uses in mind other than just the program under evaluation. That is, portions of the application are specifically intended at the time of design or writing to be used and supported in other applications, perhaps even at other sites. Additional analysis, planning, co-ordination, and design is required to meet the unique needs of the other programs or processing sites.

11. *Conversion and installation ease* increases the difficulty of application development but reduces the number and severity of problems in testing and implementation. This factor may be evidenced by the presence of a well-designed conversion or installation plan which was fully tested and modified as necessary during the system test phase. Installations performed on the fly (which usually translates to "winging it"), regardless of apparent ease, do not meet this standard.

12. *Operational ease* is not the same as end user efficiency. This factor, like the previous, requires a well-defined plan that was fully tested and modified as necessary during the system test phase. Its purpose is to provide effective but easy startup, backup, error recovery, and shutdown procedures, and to minimize such manual activities as mounting tapes or special forms, handling paper, or responding to requests for information at the operator console.

13. When the application has been specifically designed, developed, and supported for installation at *multiple sites*, for multiple organizations, additional co-ordination, review, and approval is required even if no site-unique code needs to be written. This factor may be distinguished from code reusability, in which only *some* of the application will contribute to a new and different program, perhaps only at the writing site; with multiple-site installation planning, the same application will be used at all sites. Any differences in business functions provided between the various sites would be accounted for in step one, business functions identification, not in this step, which is concerned with the application and production environment complexity as a whole.

14. When the application has been specifically designed, developed, and supported to *facilitate change*, it requires increased attention to and planning for future maintenance and modification needs. For example, business information subject to change—such as tax rates and shipping costs—is organized into tables easily accessed and maintained by the user rather than hard-coded and scattered throughout the program. As another example, providing a flexible query capability facilitates future change because stored data or information is more easily identified as needing maintenance.

To review, you may count only those factors which:

* clearly benefit the user,
* are specifically approved by the user, and
* influence to a measurable degree the design, development, implementation, or support of an application.

IFPUG is currently working very hard to augment and to standardize the 14 physical-system production environment complexity factors, or General Application Characteristics. Whereas the original definitions do require both some additional detail and some technological update, it would be a *serious mistake* for your shop not to use them as stated and weighted. A great deal of research (perhaps not readily apparent and in any case not financially or expertly feasible to the great and vast majority of MIS shops to produce alternative rules) was done to determine the 14 factors which have the greatest influence, and the correct adjustment factor for each.

Do not try to develop your own list of factors, or definitions, or weights! They probably *will not work*.

Instead, accept and use these 14. They *do* work, so don't monkey with them!

Just as were business functions classified by complexity, so are production environment factors classified by complexity or, more generally, the amount of influence they have on the application as a whole. To classify these adjustment factors, each is weighted from 0 to 5. If a factor is absent or has no influence, it is given a 0. If it heavily influences a system, increasing its difficulty to develop, implement, or support, it is given a 5. As suggested by Unisys, values between 0 and 5 are scaled according to the percentage by which the factor either affects or is required by the application. This is shown in Figures 22 and 23.

FIGURE 22.   Production Environment Processing Complexity Factors Influence Scale (except Factor 10).

Factor Value	System Influence	Per cent affects or is required by application
0	None	0%
1	Minor (insignificant)	1 - 20%
2	Moderate	21 - 40%
3	Average	41 - 60%
4	Significant	61 - 80%
5	Strong, throughout	81 - 100%

This influence chart applies to all 14 production environment factors except #10, code reusability. For this factor, Unisys suggests the following percentages apply:

FIGURE 23.   Production Environment Processing Complexity Factor 10
Influence Scale.

Factor Value	Per cent of code designed for reuse elsewhere
0	0 - 10%
1	11 - 20%
2	21 - 30%
3	31 - 40%
4	41 - 50%
5	> 50%

With this one exception, note that production environment processing complexity factors are all classified according to the same scale, unlike business functions we studied earlier. These factors should always be evaluated as follows:

1. Identify as precisely as possible the per cent by which the factor affects or is required by an application in a given production environment, then
2. Assign the appropriate value.

By using this two-step method, you will achieve greater precision because:

- You must more accurately evaluate the degree of influence by 101-point numeric scale instead of 6-value qualitative;
- Mean-value problems are avoided; without the use of determining percentages, a function point analyst would consistently rate "average" values as 3, whereas the true average, or mean, value is really 2.5. As we shall soon see, this problem alone could unnecessarily introduce an error of up to 7%—but can be entirely and easily avoided by determining factor values only by per cents and not by subjective descriptions; and
- Halo-effect value skews are less likely with a more precise numeric scale than with only subjective descriptions; data processing specialists tend to rank these adjustment factors substantially higher than reality supports. Nevertheless, there *may* be *some* occasions in which a more descriptive, though less numeric, yardstick may be applied. For those situations, the Handbook (GUIDE International Publication GPP-134) provides the following qualitative weighting factors (you may wish to combine these with the multiples-of-20% ones seen earlier).

1. *Data Communications:*

0 Application is pure batch processing.

1-2 Remote printing and/or remote data entry.

3-5 Interactive teleprocessing (TP).

3 TP front-end to a batch process.

5 Application is dominantly interactive TP.

2. *Distributed Function:*

0 Application does not aid the transfer of data or processing function between components of the system.

1 Application prepares data for end-user processing on another component of the system.

2-4 Data is prepared for transfer, is transferred, and is processed on another component of the system.

5 Processing functions are dynamically performed on the most appropriate component of the system.

3. *Performance:*

0-3 Performance analysis and design considerations are standard. No special performance requirements are stated by the user.

4 Performance analysis tasks are included in the design phase to meet stated user performance requirements.

5 In addition, performance analysis tools are used in the design, development, and/or installation phases to meet stated user performance requirements.

4. *Heavily-Used Configuration:*

0-3 Typical application run on standard production machine. No stated operation restrictions.

4 Stated operation restrictions require special constraints on the application in the central processor.

5 In addition, there are special constraints on the application in distributed components of the system.

5. *Transaction Rates:*

0-3 Transaction rates are such that performance analysis considerations are standard.

4 Performance analysis tasks are included in the design phase to meet high transaction rates stated by the user in the application requirements or service level agreement.

5 In addition, performance analysis tools are used in the design, development, and/or installation phases to meet high transaction rates stated by the user in the application requirements or service level agreement.

6. *On-line Data Entry*:

0-2 None to 15% of the transactions are interactive data entry.

3-4 15% to 30% of the transactions are interactive data entry.

  5 30% to 50% of the transactions are interactive data entry.

7. *Design for End User Efficiency*:

0-3 No stated special user requirements concerning end-user efficiency.

  4 Design tasks for human-factor considerations are included in the design phase to meet stated user requirements.

  5 In addition, special tools—like prototyping—are used to promote end user efficiency.

8. *On-line Update*:

  0 None.

1-2 On-line update of control files. Volume of updating is low and recovery is easy.

  3 On-line update of major logical internal files/information groups.

  4 In addition, protection against data loss is essential.

  5 In addition, high volumes bring cost considerations into recovery considerations.

9. *Complex Processing*:

Which of the following characteristics apply to the application?

- Extensive logical and/or mathematical processing.
- Complex processing to handle all input possibilities (multiple media or logic paths for an input).
- Complex processing to handle all output possibilities (multiple media, sorts, or distribution for an output).

- Much exception processing, many incomplete transactions, and much reprocessing of transactions.
- Sensitive control and/or security processing.

Score as:

0 None of the above applies.

1 Any one of the above applies.

2 Any two of the above apply.

3 Any three of the above apply.

4 Any four of the above apply.

5 Any five of the above apply.

10. *Usable in Other Applications*:

0-1 The application is tailored for the needs of one user organization.

2-3 Application used or produced common modules that considered more than one user's needs.

4-5 In addition, the application was specifically packaged and/or documented to facilitate re-use.

11. *Installation Ease*:

0-1 No special conversion and installation considerations were stated by the user.

2-3 Conversion and installation requirements were stated by the user, and conversion and installation guides were provided and tested.

4-5 In addition, conversion and installation tools were provided and tested.

12. *Operational Ease*:

0 No special operational considerations were stated by the user.

1-2 Effective startup, backup, and recovery processes were required, provided, and tested.

3-4 In addition, the application minimizes the need for manual activities, such as tape mounts and paper handling.

5 Application is designed for unattended operation.

13. *Multiple Sites*:

0 No user requirement to consider the needs of more than one user site.

1-3 Needs of multiple sites were considered in the design.

4-5 Documentation and support plan are provided and tested to support the application at multiple sites.

14. *Facilitate Change*:

0 No special user requirement to design the application to minimize or facilitate change.

1-3 Flexible query capability is provided.

4-5 In addition, control data is kept in tables that are maintained by the user with on-line interactive processes.

Now that each of the 14 production environment processing complexity factors has been correctly classified, the next step is to total them. When totalled, they will give a value—known as the Total Degree of Influence—between 0 and 70 (= 14 * 5). This adjustment factor total represents a ± 35% impact on the raw function point total we calculated in step 1. More precisely, the final *adjusted* function point total is equal to:

Total unadjusted, or raw, function points (from step 1)
times
(0.65 + 1% of the total degree of influence from step 2).

For example, suppose we found the raw function point total to be 1000. If all 14 adjustment factors were equal to 5, that is, a total degree of influence equal to 70, the adjusted function point total would be 1000 * (0.65 + (.01 * 70)) = 1350 function points. If all 14 adjustment factors were equal to 0, the adjusted function point total would be 1000 * (0.65 + (.01 * 0)) = 650 function points. Note again from these examples the impact, up to 35%, of the production environment on the application's point total. The average impact would be no impact. This would occur when the total degree of influence was equal to 35—the average between 0 and 70 (and also, as things turn out, a conservative on-line value; batch systems, on the other hand, may average as low as 15). In our example, both the raw and the final function point count would then equal 1000 because the 14 adjustment factors would on average have no influence on the system. The actual value for your production environment would, of course, depend on its characteristics and your system's design and performance objectives; the multiplier values ("Adjustment Factor") just given (1.0 for on-line and 0.8 for batch systems) represent conservative (low end) values and are for guideline purposes only. Note that raw function point totals calculated in step 1 do *not* change when implemented and executed in a different production environment, and that some adjustment factors *are likely* to change—but by coincidence may not change or may balance out to no net change.

Let us now return to the on-line parts system in which we earlier identified and classified business functions totalling 70 (raw) function points. We must now determine the degree of influence each of these 14 factors has on the application in the intended production environment and from this determine the final function point total. Please review the requirements definition report and system design specifications provided earlier and study the following additional specifications:

1. Response time for all on-line displays should not exceed two seconds for 95% of all requests and should never exceed ten seconds for the remaining 5%.
2. The expected transaction rate is high and the existing computer facility is of limited capacity; additionally, disk space is becoming increasingly crowded.
3. No additional hardware will be supplied to implement the system, which must not disrupt other production applications. Three-level systems testing will be performed before implementation.
4. The proposed system will be used by three internal divisions and also made available to distributors.
5. The system must be easy to use and to operate unattended in normal state; complete testing of all operational aspects must be performed to ensure smooth operation.
6. Since the system will later accommodate the entire Parts Master File, it must be easy to change and enhance.

Recall the multiples-of-20% scaling factors for production environment influences discussed earlier. Using these as a guide, we would classify the 14 on-line parts system production environment processing complexity factors as follows:

1. *Data communications:* 3. An on-line system always implies data communications, even if only local terminals are involved. Although both distributors and three internal divisions will use the system, no extensive data communications facilities are needed.

2. *Distributed data or processing:* 0. No mention is made of any distributed data or processing requirements. Terminals will be used only for data entry, inquiries, and report requests; they will neither store nor process data locally. Conversely, the indirect access to the Parts Master File does not qualify as distributed data or processing, either, because it is stored, processed, and maintained on the same processing and storage system as is its subset used in the on-line system.

3. *Application performance objectives:* 5. Recall the limited capacity of the computer and the high transaction rate. Yet, the desired response time—less than two seconds for 95% of all requests—is quite fast, especially for this environment. To be sure, creating a subset of the Parts Master File helps support this fast response time because fewer parts and other data items need be searched. But offsetting this is the additional disk space and input/output required to access the subset while other applications access the main file for essentially the same information. In an already tight or crowded configuration, such duplication increases the difficulty by which already high performance objectives may be achieved; whereas such fast response time would always represent at least significant influence, a 4, in this environment it represents strong, a 5.

4. *Heavily used, tight, or crowded configuration:* 5. We have just seen indications that the existing computer facility is bogged down and perhaps running out of gas. However, no additional hardware will be provided to implement the new system or even to alleviate current bottlenecks. Consequently, much care must be taken in system design and programming to minimize storage access routines and swapping code segments in and out of main memory.

5. *High transaction rate:* 4. Although described as "high," the transaction rate for this system does not warrant a 5 because transmissions are not continuous (as they would be in, say, a record-entry operation—even though much of the cost-benefit analysis would depend on increased efficiencies processing low-overhead/high-turnover stock items), the number of terminals is not excessive, and the amount of information transmitted on any screen is small. When evaluating a given production environment, always consider the possibility the same factor may have even stronger influence in another environment and temper your rating accordingly—that is, do not always rate such words as "high," "fast," etc. as a 5 because other environments may indicate factors that are higher, faster, etc.

6. *On-line inquiry and data entry:* 3. On-line capabilities are always more difficult to implement than batch. This system, however, represents about the simplest possible, so we give it the minimum on-line value of 3.

7. *End user efficiency:* 2. Only moderate provisions have been designed for "user friendliness" and for "learner friendliness." Although the screens are neat and well-designed, and provide a few brief prompts and error messages, they are not conversational and do not include additional help messages or screens. Also, the limited number of error messages may indicate a similarly limited number of error traps and exception handling routines. For example, one error message for the Parts Inventory Display screen is, "Invalid location-ID". A more user-friendly system would also respond, "Valid entries are 1, 2, 3, and 5 only. Please re-enter correct location and retransmit request". Longer messages might be placed on a separate help screen; handy reference to the size-code table might also be placed on-line in such a screen for review *before* the request is first transmitted.

8. *On-line update of files and data sets:* 3. In our discussion of on-line inquiry and data entry (#6), we saw that these on-line functions are more difficult to implement than batch. The same is true for on-line updates of files and data sets, for reasons mentioned earlier in this chapter. But as was also true with this system's on-line inquiry and data entry capabilities, the on-line update function is about the simplest possible—parts may only be added to or removed from the Parts Selection Table—so we give it, too, the minimum on-line value of 3. Only the keys to the Parts Master File are maintained and modified, not the detail records.

9. *Complex processing:* 1. The only situation in which this on-line parts system requires greater than average difficulty in logic, file, calculation, or exception processing is the reprocessing of incomplete or incorrect transactions, and the multiple output distribution considerations. But as a whole, processing routines are not very complex at all.

10. *Code reusability:* 0. Although this application requires easy transition to accommodate later the complete Parts Master File, none of its routines, subroutines, or other procedures will be used in any other system, or at any other site. Thus, no additional analysis, compromise, planning, or design is required. Note, however, that the code for this system must be substantially the same as the eventual full-scale system. Because these two systems are essentially the same throughout the organization—differentiated only by the size of the file searched— and not different applications, this design factor is more properly handled by factor 14, the ability to facilitate change, and by factor 13, multiple-site installation, than by this factor.

11. *Conversion and installation ease:* 2. We must give credit for the installation plan devised, including its request for three-level (unit, link or string, and systems) testing before implementation. Because, however, of the system's simplicity, only moderate difficulty is expected during this phase. No conversion requirement has been specified (because no new hardware will be purchased) and the required installation ease of the future, full-scale parts system is once again more properly handled by factor 14, the ability to facilitate change.

12. *Operational ease:* 5. The requirements definition report tells us the new system must be easy to use and to operate (unattended). All operational aspects, from startup to output distribution or error recovery, will be tested to ensure the plan is complete and operates smoothly.

13. *Multiple site installation:* 5. From the requirements definition report we know the on-line system will be used by three internal divisions and by various distributors. This increases the amount of necessary coordination, review, and approval because each site representative will probably have a different idea of what information is needed and how it should be presented—even if no site-unique features are included in the system. All users of the new system will be served by the same application. The increased difficulty in design compromise, development, and support must be claimed here and not under factor 10, code reusability; factor 10 would be reserved for the situation in which the systems installed in the various sites are all substantially different, yet derived from this one on-line parts system which at the time of its design took this into full account.

14. *Facilitate change:* 4. We have already discussed the system's ability to facilitate change when evaluating both the code reusability and the conversion/installation ease factors. Both of these factors were rated with respect to the present system, not the future. No code was to be reused elsewhere and no conversion was planned. The installation plan referred to the present on-line system, not the future enhanced version. Thus, the ability to facilitate change and enhancement is properly claimed here. Despite heavy emphasis in the requirements definition report, we cannot rate this factor higher than a 4 because when the time comes to implement the full-scale parts system, much of this smaller version must be torn out and patched—especially the add and remove inputs, the Parts Selection Table, and the Selected-Parts File, which also includes the batch interface and the control report. It cannot be done with our on-line parts system, but stubbing out the hooks into the to-be-added-later procedures would facilitate change to a degree of 5.

We have now completed our analysis of how the anticipated production environment will affect the planned on-line parts system. For ready reference, we may list our values on the Summary Sheet as shown in Figure 24.

FIGURE 24.   On-Line Parts System Processing Complexity Factors.

Processing Complexity Factors			
Factor	Value	Factor	Value
1. Data communications	3	8. On-line update	3
2. Distributed data or processing	0	9. Complex compressing	1
3. Performance objectives	5	10. Code reusability	0
4. Tight configuration	5	11. Conversion/installation ease	2
5. High transaction rate	4	12. Operational ease	5
6. On-line inquiry/data entry	3	13. Multiple site installation	5
7. End user efficiency	2	14. Facilitate change	4
		TOTAL DEGREE OF INFLUENCE	42

The complete Summary Sheet for our on-line parts system would look as shown in Figure 25.

FIGURE 25. On-Line Parts System: Complete Summary Sheet.

Business Function	Number	Complexity		Factor		Line Total	Group Total
OUTPUTS	2	Simple	*	4	=	8	
	2	Average	*	5	=	10	
	0	Complex	*	7	=	0	
TOTAL:	4						18
INQUIRIES	3	Simple	*	4	=	12	
	0	Average	*	5	=	0	
	0	Complex	*	6	=	0	
	0	Complex	*	7	=	0	
TOTAL:	3						12
INPUTS	3	Simple	*	3	=	9	
	0	Average	*	4	=	0	
	0	Complex	*	6	=	0	
TOTAL:	3						9
FILES	3	Simple	*	7	=	21	
	0	Average	*	10	=	0	
	0	Complex	*	15	=	0	
TOTAL:	3						21
INTERFACES	2	Simple	*	5	=	10	
	0	Average	*	7	=	0	
	0	Complex	*	10	=	0	
TOTAL:	2						10

TOTAL UNADJUSTED FUNCTION POINTS: 70

Processing Complexity Factors

Factor	Value	Factor	Value
1. Data communications	3	8. On-line update	3
2. Distributed data or processing	0	9. Complex processing	1
3. Performance objectives	5	10. Code reusability	0
4. Tight configuration	5	11. Implementation/installation ease	2
5. High transaction rate	4	12. Operational ease	5
6. On-line inquiry/data entry	3	13. Multiple site installation	5
7. End user efficiency	2	14. Facilitate change	4
		TOTAL DEGREE OF INFLUENCE	42

FINAL CALCULATIONS

1. *Adjustment Factor:* $0.65 + (0.01 * 42) = 1.07$

2. *Final Function Point Count:* $70 * 1.07 = \underline{\ \ 75\ \ }$ Function Points

Total raw FP count

Note the effect of the production environment on the raw function point total calculated earlier. For the on-line parts system, the raw total of 70 is multiplied by the adjustment factor, 1.07, to yield a final function point count of 75. This 7% increase is in accordance with expected on-line values; the 1.0 adjustment factor mentioned earlier, you will recall, is only a suggested minimum value for an on-line system. In any case, this 75 FP value accurately and quantitatively measures this system's size and evaluates its business value to the end user. *Appreciate fully this*: At this point, only about *5%* of project duration has elapsed (if the designed screens are not included) or less than *50%* of project duration (if screens are included)—yet the accuracy *far exceeds* any other metric available, *none* of which is usable until after the code is completely written, or at *95%* project duration. They cannot even forecast the remaining *5%* as accurately as FPA could forecast the remaining *95%* in most cases. The only methodology more accurate than FPA is gazing into your crystal ball, if you have one...

Although as systems go it is very small, the methods used in its analysis and evaluation are precisely the same as would be used in a larger system. Thus, you may review this system's evaluation procedures with confidence as you tackle more complex systems, such as...*your* turn now!—the Personnel System!

4

Personnel System FPA Exercise: Function Point Counting from a Requirements Definition Report

Read carefully the following requirements definition report for a planned personnel system. It is recommended that you read the entire report before you attempt to identify and classify business functions and production environment factors. After you have read the report and gained a big-picture appreciation of the application, re-read the document and begin searching for business function groups, beginning with outputs and inquiries and continuing with inputs, files, and interfaces. After classifying the business functions you found, repeat the process for all 14 production environment complexity factors. Then do it again. Probe and dig for more. Remember it is more important to list a function than to classify it, but overlooking functions—especially in early development stages, when functions may not be so obvious—is the main cause of error. Never assume the documentation or even sample reports, inquiries, or inputs to be complete (are they ever?); rather, ask the user for clarification and amplification as necessary (you need not do this for this exercise!). *Appreciate* that these requirements are written *very early* in the project cycle—usually after only about 5% of total project duration and budget expenditure; no other methodology can give this early, yet still this accurate, a forecast of system size and value! True, as the project proceeds, more clarity will be provided—and more "bells and whistles." This is normal and should be expected. In the example provided in the GUIDE International GPP-134 Handbook, the project grew from 245 raw function points (262 adjusted) to 350 raw function points (375 adjusted)—a significant gain of 43%. *The problem was incomplete or insufficient detail,* not the FPA methodology. No other method could do better, and this early a notice will prevent you from "selling the farm."

"The kind of predictor that is measurable early in a project is *never* as strongly correlated to eventual results as the predictors that become available later." - DeMarco.

The user will appreciate such attention to detail and avoiding misunderstandings later on. Count only those business functions specifically approved by the user. The only exception to this is when a *vital* function (such as file backup or recovery) has been omitted from the requirements definition report. In this situation, bring the matter to the user's attention and count the function unless the user specifically requests its omission (be absolutely certain to get his or her autograph in this case!).

Work carefully. Review and critically analyze your work when done. Have fun, good luck, and—careful counting! A suggested solution to this exercise may be found at the end of this book. The values provided will probably be different— but should not be much different—from the values you determine. This solution is a composite of answers provided by University of Auckland Professor Eberhard E. Rudolph, 14 Unisys software consultants, one incredibly fine teacher (M. Kay Schimanski of Unisys), 73 master's-level and upper-division students in 4 (including Boeing) of my university classes, and myself. Still, these are "EPA estimates," not actuals. Your answer will, of course, vary somewhat as a function of the underlying design—still, it should not vary by more than 10% of the solution total because the majority of features are straightforward in both identification and classification. Remember, only 5% of project budget has been expended at this point; other methodologies—requiring counts of already-produced code lines or metrics—could not be employed until the code is written, or the 95% time mark (and probably 295% of budget!). As more detail is provided, and features added— or if these had been included in *this* document—Function Point Analysis can, even at this early time, arrive at a far more accurate estimate in lookahead mode than can the others (even in hindsight!).

PERSONNEL SYSTEM:
REQUIREMENTS DEFINITION REPORT
Courtesy of: Professor Eberhard E. Rudolph, University Of Auckland

I. SUMMARY

The purpose of this report is to define the major business functions to be performed by the personnel system in sufficient detail to be fully reviewed and understood by the key personnel functional areas before the start of actual design. This report can then act as the baseline document against which results and change can be measured during design and implementation of the personnel system.

Eleven major business functions are to be provided by the system:

Add or Reactivate an Individual
Change an Individual's Job
Process a Compensation Action
Change an Individual's Organizational Assignment
Change an Individual's Personnel Status
Update an Individual's Personal Data
Make an Inquiry
Correct Data
Change Security Data Base Parameters
Maintain Tables
Produce Reports and Other Outputs

Further, there will be four special processes important to several of these functions; these are described in this report as they apply to particular functions. They are: change a key, delete a record, change historical data, and make a mass change.

II. SYSTEM OBJECTIVES

1. Provide enhanced capabilities for meeting operational and corporate needs for human resource information required in decision making, with improvement in the timeliness, accuracy, and accessibility of needed information.

2. Reduce the unnecessary overhead and costs associated with maintaining the large number of separate computer systems existing today.

3. Reduce the costs of operating management in their personnel decision-making by providing them with more complete and useful information.

4. Improve productivity throughout the company in personnel management and administrative functions by relieving areas of the need to manually maintain and manage information and retrieve it from multiple sources.

5. Consolidate the number of documents and streamline procedures required to administer personnel functions.

6. Provide a flexible system capability for quickly responding to new and anticipated requirements.

III. SYSTEM CHARACTERISTICS

1. On-line inquiry, entry, and real-time update. This will take place through terminals in the operating areas.

2. Easy-to-use information retrieval language. To meet the timely and flexible needs for special information requests, there will be a retrieval language which gives non-data-processing personnel the capability to design, write, and run straightforward reports.

3. Timeliness of information and reports. Personnel data will be more current since it will be updated daily under the personnel system. The same-day turnaround time anticipated from the information retrieval system also will improve current response time.

4. User control of data. Operating areas will be responsible for entry into the system, or in special circumstances, for originating the forms and profiles which add or change personnel records and sending them to the personnel department.

5. Provision for maintaining historical data. History required by corporate functions and legal requirements will start with current job and compensation data and then accumulate as future transactions take place.

6. Compatibility with the existing teleprocessing network. Compatibility is planned in order to utilize terminals already in place. Only a small number of terminals will actually have to be purchased for the personnel system.

7. Extensive use of tables. The personnel system will employ tables and logic within the system to increase accuracy, reduce update time, and facilitate maintenance.

8. Modular design, flexibility, and adaptability. Since the design of the system is modular, later phases and enhancements can be developed as separate projects. System design will provide the flexibility to respond to new requirements in a timely fashion.

9. Interfaces with the existing payroll system. There is an interface with the existing payroll system. Certain data common to both the new personnel system file and the existing payroll files will flow first into the personnel system and be passed to the existing payroll system. While the existing payroll system will receive this common personnel data from the personnel system, it will retain an override capability for last-minute updates to those fields in its own files in order to prevent adverse impact on payroll processing.

10. Security, audit controls, privacy, and confidentiality. Because of the sensitive nature of personnel information, the personnel system will provide protection from unauthorized file accesses. Levels of security will be established according to the need to know items of information on various sets of the company population. System audit and control reports will be automatically prepared to verify that all data changes have been input to the system and processed by each step of the system.

IV. SUMMARY OF PERSONAL RECORD UPDATE PROCESSING

When the system is installed, the primary input media for personnel data will be screens on remote terminals for direct data entry by managers of operational areas and their designated representatives. An authorized individual (operator) at his or her terminal will select the input screen for the function desired from a general menu of functions. The operator will key in the required data to initiate the transaction.

In exceptional circumstances, Personnel Profiles will be accepted by the personnel department for entry of personnel data changes. Where Personnel Profiles are used, the responsible party will cross out on the Profile the personnel information to be changed and print the new personnel information above it in the space provided on the Profile's action copy (or, if no information is displayed, simply print the new personnel information inside the the appropriate block). The area will separate the action copy from the file copy and then route the former in a secure and confidential manner directly to the personnel department. The area will retain the file copy for use in verifying the accuracy of the new Profile and for reference until the updated Profile is received. The personnel department will audit the action copy for accuracy and then input the data on its terminals to the personnel system.

1. Validity and consistency at on-line entry

Validity and consistency checks will be performed on-line after the operator has completed keying in the data and prior to processing the transaction into the system. The input screen will check the data entered to ensure that

- Every field entered contains legitimate values (matches some allowable value, contains all numeric characters, etc.); and
- Certain relationships between two or more data elements are observed.

When a record is being changed, the system will check the data entered to ensure that an active personnel record exists for the Social Security Number entered. When a record is being added, the system will check the data entered to ensure that no active personnel record exists for the Social Security Number entered.

During validity and consistency, the Table Data Base will be accessed to look up descriptive code tables for validation criteria. System-generated error messages will point out exceptions to the checks. A terminal operator's manual will explain in detail how to react to these conditions. Fields which are designated by the user as fatal will cause the transaction to fail at the point of entry. When the information is being keyed by a personnel department operator, the operator will have to call the submitting area to correct the field in error. Other fields may generate warning messages which will allow processing to continue even if not corrected immediately.

2. Processing to the suspense data base

After acceptance by on-line validity and consistency, transactions will be transmitted to the Suspense Data Base and stored (sorted by organization). Those with future effective dates will be stored until their effective date. A program will search for duplicate entries (two entries with the same Social Security Number and Transaction Code) and report them with a warning message.

3. Updating the personnel data base

Transactions on the Suspense Data Base will be applied to the Personnel Data Base in a batch run when the effective date is equal to or less than (before) the run date. Incoming transactions to the Personnel Data Base will be processed through an update program which will test certain relationships and previous validity and consistency checks in the event changes in procedures, acceptable values, etc., have taken place between processing to the Suspense Data Base and updating the Personnel Data Base. An update to a personnel record will in turn create historical information.

4. Interface with the existing payroll system

Updates which change an individual's job, compensation, status, or organizational assignment will require an interface with the existing payroll system. An interface program module will prepare payroll transaction codes related to Personnel System Transactions for the existing payroll system. Accurate and efficient payroll processing absolutely depends upon correct Personnel Data Base data. Validity tests will be at least as stringent as those performed currently in the two payroll systems on the relevant data elements.

5. *Outputs*

Personnel record creation and update will be associated with the following outputs:

  a. Transaction Code Files for existing payroll system
  b. Personnel Profiles
  c. Action Reports
  d. Notification Reports
  e. Error Reports
  f. Audit and Control Reports

See Appendix B for a description of these outputs.

V. MAJOR BUSINESS FUNCTIONS

A. Add or Reactivate an Individual

1. *Input*

There is not an exact match between a hire or rehire and a personnel system Add or Reactivate Transaction. A rehire from the point of view of the employment area will be an Add from the point of view of the personnel system when that person's prior service predates the personnel system. (Implementation will assemble records on all individuals current on computer files at the time of implementation, so that an individual who terminated before implementation would cause a personnel system Add Transaction upon rehire.) Conversely, there are situations in which a hire from the point of view of the employment area would be a Reactivation for the personnel system. In addition, if an individual has two organizational assignments at once, the second would be a hire for the employment area, but an additional organizational assignment for the personnel system. Determination of the transaction type, therefore, will be internal to the personnel system: All hires and rehires will be handled by entering the Hire Screens. The employment areas will be responsible for determining the Adjusted Entry Date.

2. *Process*

a) Change the master record

There are three situations the personnel system will handle for the Add or Reactivate function: Add an Individual, Reactivate an Individual, and Add an Additional Organizational Assignment. Which of these functions will be performed in a given case will be determined automatically by the computer system.

Add an individual. In this case, the personnel system has no record of the individual. Either the person has never been associated with the company or terminated prior to the personnel system implementation. The system will add the Individual's Identification Data, Education, Previous Work Experience, Major Organizational Assignment, Specific Organizational Data, and Compensation Data.

Reactivate an individual's record. A record exists for the person but the person has terminated. If the person is returning to the same major organization from which he or she terminated, the individual's Identification Data and Major Organizational Assignment data are changed to active status. Otherwise, the identification data is changed to active status and new organizational data and compensation data are added.

If the effective date on the hiring form is in the future, the transaction will update the Suspense Data Base for processing when the person reports for work; otherwise, if the effective date is the current date or past, the transaction will update the Personnel Data Base.

b) Interface with the existing payroll system

The personnel system will carry a table of unused payroll identification numbers for the existing payroll system and will assign the new person the next available number, which will be printed on the Personnel Profile. Reactivated personnel will be reassigned their original number if it is available.

c) Outputs

Using the Add or Reactivate an Individual function will cause the initial personnel profile to be produced for the appropriate personnel functional areas and for the person's organizational assignment area. If transactions have been entered to the Suspense Data Base, the employment areas will be notified of pending additions. Those employment areas that require them will receive weekly reports listing personnel added or reactivated.

B. Change an Individual's Job

1. Input

For the personnel system, a job represents a set of activities performed in one or more positions at the same level. Each current job will be assigned a unique Job Number. In the future, the creation of new jobs or the re-evaluation of existing jobs will require the addition of new Job Numbers. A change in job is specified to the personnel system by a change in Job Number.

Job Tables. The personnel system will have Job Tables for all jobs. Maintenance of these tables will be the responsibility of the operating areas. Information on these tables will be common to a job and thus apply to multiple incumbents. A change in the table (items can be added, changed, or deleted at any time) could affect multiple individuals. Therefore, changes in elements in the Job Table will be analyzed for possible special processing of mass changes to the records of individuals affected.

This transaction will be used when there is a job change exclusive of any accompanying change in organizational assignment and/or compensation level.

For a change in job only, the primary item which the operator must enter will be the Job Table key, the Job Number. All other information associated with that Job Number will be automatically extracted from the Job Table. This will reduce effort and assure consistency. Certain elements extracted from the table will be capable of being overridden. Other elements will not be able to be changed.

Job change transactions often occur in conjunction with and on the same effective date as other changes, most notably changes in compensation or organizational assignment. In such cases, the changes will be entered as a single action. Where an organizational transfer is also involved with the job change, the sending department will initiate the change, that is, they will obtain and enter the new Job Number and Organizational Assignment Number.

2. Process

a) Change the master record

No change in Job Transactions will be updated to the Personnel Data Base until they are both properly authorized and their effective date has arrived.

b) Interface with the existing payroll system.

C. Process a Compensation Action (only)

1. Input

Compensation actions often occur in conjunction with (on the same effective date as) other changes, most notably changes in job, organizational assignment, and sometimes personnel status. Therefore, the following types of transactions must be accepted:

a) Change in compensation only

b) Change in compensation and job (promotion and demotion)

c) Change in compensation, job, and organizational assignment (promotion and transfer)

d) Change in compensation and personnel status (hourly to salaried and salaried to hourly).

For cases b, c, and d, there are screens for entering new compensation, job, personnel status, and organizational assignment data, chained together if necessary. When a compensation action is precipitated by other changes on the same effective date, the changes will be entered as a single action. The following types of compensation actions will be accepted by the personnel system:

- Update granted increase amounts and types
- Update hours per week
- Update merit rating.

Any or all of the above updates can be processed on the same screen(s). Each update (except merit rating) will be associated with an effective date on which the transaction, if authorized, will be processed. Operators will only enter those fields that need to be changed or input for the first time; derived fields, like seniority, will automatically be displayed.

2. Process

a) Change the master record

No change in compensation fields on the Personal Data Base will occur until the Compensation Action Transactions are properly authorized and their effective date has arrived. There will be Authorization Indicator fields on the Compensation Action Transactions on the Suspense Data Base that can only be activated by certain security passwords, held by individuals with personnel authorization for compensation actions and the personnel department (when policy allows delegation of personnel authorization below current levels, this can be accommodated through the Personnel System Security System). It is from the Suspense Data Base that various miscellaneous reports will be generated and distributed for proper action (authorization) prior to any changes actually affecting the Personnel Data Base.

b) Interface with the existing payroll system

c) Special processes

   (i) Mass changes will be handled as determined by the number of individuals affected. Smaller numbers can be handled as normal. However, substantial input probably will require further analysis to determine whether the change should in fact affect all the potential candidates.

   (ii) Incentives and special payment information will be passed to the personnel system from the payroll system on an annual basis. This information will become part of an individual's compensation record; however, it will not appear on the individual's Personnel Profile.

   (iii) Annual Merit Pool and Bi-Weekly Salary Action Report. The personnel system procedures for these processes will attempt to make these tasks more timely and effective for operational managers and Personnel Administrators. These procedures will help managers focus more closely on the job of annual salary planning and budget control.

      All modifications, deletions and additions should be made on the Bi-Weekly Salary Action Reports. These reports will go to the personnel department, which will update each individual's Suspense Data Base Authorization Indicator so that the entry can update the Personnel Data Base on the effective date.

3. Output

Bi-Weekly Salary Action Reports
These reports can be used by the personnel department as an internal report to display what compensation actions are to occur before the next pay cycle. This will allow them to follow up on any transactions that have not been authorized, yet are supposed to become effective on the approaching payroll cycle. Also, since compensation actions are so critical, all will appear on these reports, even those that pass all validity and consistency checks.

D. Change an Individual's Organizational Assignment

1. Input

For the personnel system, an Organizational Assignment identifies the lowest level administrative unit to which an individual belongs. Movement within or out of the Organizational Assignment will represent a transfer. Each administrative unit will be assigned a unique Organizational Assignment Number. A transfer would then be denoted to the personnel system by a change in Organizational Assignment Number. Organizational Assignment Number changes will occur independently or could be precipitated by other changes (in job or compensation).

For initiating an Organizational Assignment change, the primary item which the operator must enter will be the Organizational Assignment Table key, the Organizational Assignment Number. All other information associated with that Organizational Assignment Number will be automatically extracted from the Organizational Assignment Table. This will reduce effort and assure consistency. Capability would be provided to transfer a large number of individuals automatically, either by submitting one input transaction or by a table change.

2. Process

Depending on the structure of the Personnel Data Base, various update keys will be employed for the purpose of changing an individual's Organizational Assignment; for example, Social Security Number and Organizational Assignment Number will be part of the personnel system update key.

a) Change the master record

All Organizational Assignment processing will be initiated using an Organizational Assignment Effective Date, which must contain the necessary date information to satisfy validity and consistency requirements of interfacing systems. This Organizational Assignment Effective Date will be used as a multipurpose date, effecting the desired transaction at the proper time, and becoming the Organizational Assignment Date on the Personnel Data Base and the effective date on the respective interface systems. Depending on the transaction's Organizational Assignment Effective Date, the transaction will update the on-line Personnel Data Base (providing proper authorization was received) or be moved to the Suspense Data Base for future initiation, providing it passes personnel system validity and consistency checks at the time of entry. Should the Organizational Assignment change not be independent, but instead be precipitated by another change, the complete set of transactions would move simultaneously.

Organizational Assignment transactions to be effected at a future date or those needing approval will be moved to and reside in the Suspense Data Base. Capability will be provided so as to allow inquiry, corrections, changes, and deletions to transactions contained in the Suspense Data Base. Two criteria must be present to initiate an update from the Suspense Data Base to the Personnel Data Base:

- The Organizational Assignment transaction effective date must equal current personnel system process cycle, and
- If authorization of the transaction is required, the Authorization Indicator must be set to on.

A history record will be automatically generated and moved by the system at the time new information updates the Personnel Data Base. Examples of history data retained resulting from a new Organizational Assignment are:

- Prior effective date; and
- Prior Organizational Assignment Number.

History information on an Organizational Assignment most likely will be incorporated with other historical transactions taking place simultaneously. This would at least be true with respect to editing or viewing an individual's record.

b) Interface with the existing payroll system

3. Output

Organizational Assignment Action Reports will be distributed, when required, to gain the necessary authorization to effect a transaction from the appropriate individuals in an organization. Authorization Indicators will be set (approved) upon receipt in the personnel department of the signed (authorized) action report.

These reports will be sorted by organization and distributed to appropriate individuals with personnel authorization and personnel functional areas. Within the aforementioned criteria, sequencing will be at the dictate of the receiving area. Any transaction requiring an action will be displayed, as an English request, with areas provided to comply with the information requested. In this sense, this output will be considered a turnaround document.

E. Change an Individual's Personnel Status

1. Input

For the personnel system, the personnel status changes encompass many variables concerning an individual's relationship within an Organizational Assignment. The following types of Personnel Status Transactions, as they pertain to an Organizational Assignment, must be accepted:

a) Change in employment type status

b) Change in organizational assignment availability status (active or terminated)

c) Change in payroll mode of payment status (hourly to salaried and salaried to hourly)

d) Change in four day or five day status

e) Change in leave status

f) Change in union status.

2. Process

a) Change the master record

When authorization is required, no transactions will be updated to the Personnel Data Base until both they are properly authorized and their effective date has arrived. There will be Authorization Indicator fields that can only be activated by certain security password numbers held by individuals with personnel authorization for personnel status changes and the personnel department.

b) Interface with the existing payroll system

F. Change an Individual's Personal Data

1. Input

For the personnel system, personal data represents those items of information which are personal to the individual and often independent of any personnel relationship with the organization (such as emergency contact data). Further, they are items of information for which the individual will often be the source advising of the change. Consequently, there would be no need of any approval mechanism for most personal data transactions.

Should the personal data item requiring change not be displayed on the Personnel Profile, a Universal Update Form would be prepared by the appropriate personnel functional area. Routing of the Personnel Profile and/or Universal Update Form to the personnel department will be accomplished in a secure and confidential manner. Using the new data printed on the Personnel Profile or the Universal Update Form, a member of the personnel department will enter the information and effect the change.

The following personal data transactions must be accepted:

a) Change in an individual's identification data
b) Change in an individual's address or telephone data
c) Change in an individual's other personal data
d) Change in an individual's emergency contact data

An authorized individual (operator) at his or her terminal will select the input screen for the personal data function from a general menu of functions. The operator will key in the required data to effect the transaction.

2. Process

a) Change the master record

All changes to an individual's personal data will be processed against the Personnel Data Base immediately. There will be no Suspense Data Base processing associated with changes to an individual's personal data. There will be no historical requirement for personal data. Former Name will, however, be automatically updated when a specific transaction is processed to change one's name. The transaction to correct a name will not initiate an automatic update to Former Name.

b) Interface with the existing payroll system

G. Make an Inquiry

Inquiries will be of six general types:

- Show an individual's current record
- List an individual's history
- List suspense records for an individual
- List individuals' records by Organizational Assignment
- Show table data
- Show audit data.

1. Input

The operator will have a menu of the above available inquiry choices from which to choose

a) Individual's current data inquiry
b) Individual's historical data inquiry
c) Individual's suspense data inquiry
d) Organizational assignment inquiry
e) Table data base inquiry
f) Audit data base inquiry.

2. Process

There will be separate screens for each record. If the operator wants to see a single record, the system will display only that record. The only validity and consistency for inquiry transactions is that the operator is authorized to view the data and the system will ensure that the individual exists in the data base. If requested records are not present, the system will inform the operator with warning messages. If more than one record fulfills search requirements, the operator will be given a choice of which to see.

For inquiry transactions involving multiple records, the system will extract meaningful data elements and display a one-line extract on the screen for each occurrence. If there are more occurrences of the records than one screen will hold, the operator will be able to scroll and choose one of the records listed (via a line number) for a complete display.

3. Output

a) Individual's current data inquiry. This transaction will show, within the security restrictions of the operator, everything in the Personnel Data Base on the specified person. The display will begin with the Basic Personal Data screen and continue with current job information and current salary information. The operator may choose to view all information, in which all current records pertaining to the selected individual will be displayed. The operator may also choose to see only a part of the individual's information, such as current assignment information. This choice would show only data relating to current assignment.

b) Individual's historical data. The operator may list all the historical data for a person by data type. That is, the operator can view all the assignments a person has had, all the salaries, or all the education information. In each case, the data will be displayed as single-line extracts on the screen, filling as many screens as necessary to show all the data. One screen will usually be sufficient to show all the extracts; however, if the operator chooses to view complete data for a single extract line, each record type will be shown on the same format screen as current information.

c) Suspense data. These are transactions that have been entered into the personnel system but have not yet taken effect. The operator can list all the transactions that have not yet taken effect for the individual. These are displayed as one-line extracts on the screen from which the operator may choose one to view more completely or to change.

d) Organizational assignment data. Records of all individuals in an Organizational Assignment can be displayed as a screen (or screens) of one-line extracts. On individual records within organizational assignments, the operator may view all the individuals in a Cost Center, District, or Agency, and may choose Basic data, Assignment data, Compensation data, or Education data.

e) Table Data Base data. The operator may select an entry in any of the system tables—for example, the Job Table, the Table of States, or the Organizational Assignment Table. Because the kinds of tables used by the system will differ in content, the system will use multiple screen formats to display table data.

f) Audit Data Base data. Only the personnel department will be able to use this inquiry, which will display information concerning system operation. The personnel department will view entries in the Audit Data Base only as necessary to resolve unusual problems with the system, since audit and control reports will be produced daily.

H. Correct Data

A correction transaction is used to modify date-effective data in such a way that new history is not produced. In addition, it is used to modify fields which are judged to be correctable only by the personnel department or by a single operating area. Non-date-effective data items that are not specially protected can be corrected by using the change personal data transaction. If a history record is involved in a correction transaction, it may be necessary for the system to delete it.

1. Input

Input forms will be either the Universal Update Form, a corrected Personnel Profile, or action reports, which will be routed to the personnel department. Screens will consist of an initial menu together with the different kinds of corrections from which the operator will select. The operator will see the current record on the CRT screen and will simply overlay the field or fields in error. Corrections are subject to the same validity and consistency checks as other functions.

If the field being corrected is dependent upon an effective date, then this date must be included with the correction in order for the system to locate the correct field or record. These corrections will only be done by the personnel department. The following types of corrections will be available:

- Basic Personal data
- Current Assignment data
- Historical Assignment data
- Suspense items not yet processed
- Table data

2. Process

a) Change the master record. The operator will select the desired kind of correction, in some cases performing an inquiry in order to determine whether an item is on the Suspense Data Base or on the Personnel Data Base, and will provide the key for the individual's record. After validity and consistency are established, the appropriate files are updated.

- Personal data: The change is immediate; no other records are affected.
- Current Organizational Assignment: The correction is done; no other records are affected.
- Historical Assignment data: If the change is being reversed (for example, if a promotion was given to the wrong person), the current record is restored to the state it was in originally, then the history record is deleted. If the change does not affect current status, the correction will be made with no effect on other records.
- Suspense items not yet processed: If the transaction is being reversed, the record is deleted; otherwise, the change is made.

- Table data: The personnel department will evaluate the effect of the correction on historical data and will act in order to maintain correct relationships among table entries.

b) Interface with the existing payroll system. Because of expected low volumes of corrections, only a manual interface with the existing payroll system will be maintained.

I. Change Security Data Base Parameters

1. Input

The personnel system will be completely secured from unauthorized use by means of internally defined and externally adopted procedures. These procedures must be followed in a rigid manner to make the Personnel System Security System effective. However, the system must be flexible enough to meet future changes in policy or in organization. The security system must also be developed in a way that does not compromise the expected performances of the teleprocessing network. To that extent, the Personnel System Security System will be developed to use an external file (be a separate data base apart from the Personnel Data Base) containing all the control parameters that make up an individual's security definition. The parameters within the table will dictate exactly what that operator may do relative to the personnel system functions, may effect within the personnel system, and may view within the personnel system organizations.

The operational areas will work closely together with the personnel system security coordinator in the personnel department to ensure that proper procedures are followed and only the personnel system authorized users are placed on the Personnel System Security Data Base. Therefore, all procedures to initiate, change, or delete passwords or options must be in accordance with those described in current procedure writeups.

a) Security Data Base transactions
These transactions will be input to the security system by the personnel system security coordinator or a designated representative. These will be the only individuals allowed to enter the security transactions. The possible types of transactions that the personnel system security system must be able to process are:

- Add a new personnel system user
- Delete a personnel system user
- Establish authorized views

- Establish authorized personnel system functions (such as compensation actions or job changes)
- Establish authorized computer functions (like Inquiry or Update).

The above transactions will be designated on a personnel system Security Status Form which will be sent to the personnel system administrator in a secure and confidential manner. These documents will require the appropriate authorizing signature(s). When information is keyed into the system, certain specified fields will be non-displayed to provide protection against misuse.

2. Process

a) Change the Security Data Base record

Information will be validated and consistency checked against standard predetermined conventions; duplicate users are certainly not allowed, nor the deletion of an authorized user when one does exist. It may be possible to enter an effective date with any update transaction to allow the personnel system to be ready for an individual at a future date.

3. Outputs

a) Notification reports

These reports will be sent to the operational areas indicating that the security requests have been made. No passwords will appear on these reports.

b) Audit and control reports

J. Maintain Tables

1. Input

Tables will play an important role in the personnel system processing. The use of tables will facilitate data entry, data verification, and data integrity. Responsibility for ensuring that tables are correct and up-to-date will be in the users' hands. As an exception, table maintenance will be initiated by the personnel system administrator receiving a request on Table Maintenance Request Forms from a responsible user area or as a result of a system change or enhancement. These will allow the user to request several changes to the same table or to multiple tables. Table maintenance requests will require authorization in the form of a signature which will be verified in the personnel department. All table maintenance will be system-

audited by the generation of input journals and error reports which will be stored in the personnel department. The personnel department will contact users to clarify or correct any errors.

Table maintenance will be distinct from Personnel Data Base processing. Only those operators with appropriately designated security will be allowed to do table maintenance. The number of tables in the system will virtually be limitless. The tables themselves will vary in size and content and they will all reside within the personnel system Table Data Base.

   a) Table Update Transactions. The types of transactions that must be accepted for table maintenance are:

   - Add a table (batch only)
   - Delete a table
   - Change a table entry
   - Add a table entry
   - Delete a table entry
   - List the table directory
   - List table(s).

   The deletion or addition of a table will typically occur when there is a system change or enhancement (tables can only be added in batch).

2. Process

Only those operators with the appropriate security level will be allowed to update and/or list tables. After correctly logging onto the personnel system, the operator will request the table maintenance option. A menu screen will appear that will allow the operator to select the table to be updated or listed. For those transactions which will effect table entries, the appropriate input screen for each table will appear. For new entries, operators will have to put in the required information (which will immediately be validated). For those entries that are to be changed or deleted, the operator should first enter the table item key. This will display the table entry on the terminal screen. The operator can then change the fields as required or may delete the entry entirely. The operator can continue to enter changes to the current table or return to the table menu and select the next table to be updated. All errors encountered will be flagged and must be corrected before update will be accepted.

3. Output

a) Notification reports

After the tables have been changed, added, or deleted, notification reports will be produced to inform interested parties.

b) Audit and control reports

c) Table lists

K. Produce Reports and Other Outputs

1. Input

The reports produced by the personnel system primarily fall into two categories: those generated by programs within the personnel system processing cycle and those generated by programs outside the personnel system processing cycle. The first category consists of reports that are typically generated on a cyclical basis (daily, weekly, monthly, quarterly), whereas the second category are those that are generated on an ad hoc basis. Scheduled reports are those that can be either determined by a user's needs or triggered by a specific function. These reports fall into the following classes:

- Personnel profiles
- Notification reports
- Action reports
- Audit reports
- Control reports
- Specialized user reports.

Ad hoc reporting, prior to the time a user has a terminal, will occur within the personnel department. Users will express the need for a specific report and the personnel system Report Writer will determine the best way to produce the document. The tools the personnel system Report Writer will have at hand are:

- A high-level on-line query language
- A report writer package
- A statistical package.

The personnel system Report Writer will receive from the user what the request is, the priority of the request, whether the request is truly one-time, and when the user needs to see the output. This information will appear on a Report Request Form. A valid signature, which will be verified by the personnel system Report Writer, must also be on the form.

2. Process

a) Produce reports

Requestors can either follow the above procedure or, if authorized, create and submit their own queries using the high-level query language at the terminal. On-line queries will be controlled by the system so that some user requests may be routed to a batch queue to be run during the day or later that evening. This is necessary because those queries that use inordinate amounts of computer time can impact the performance of the entire on-line network. Output can be displayed at a terminal or printed either remotely or locally in a secured area.

3. Output

a) Control reports

All print requests will be logged on a control report in order to trace what, when, and who was involved in any query.

APPENDIX A
INPUT FORMS

A. THE PERSONNEL SYSTEM SECURITY STATUS FORM

Purpose: To provide the manager with a means of selecting the personnel system security options for his/her personnel.

Description: The Security Status Form will be the input document that the Security Coordinator will use to enter and update information in the personnel system security system. The operational area manager will fill out this form and return it to the personnel department. The information will describe what the user of the personnel system may do and can view. The contents of the form include: Security Clerk Code, the personnel system transactions, view parameters (like Organizational Assigments), function codes, data base segment names, and table names.

Distribution: The form is sent to the personnel department. A copy is kept in the personnel department.

Volume and Frequency: As security change requests are made.

B.   TABLE MAINTENANCE REQUEST FORM

Purpose: To provide the user with the ability to make changes to the personnel system tables.

Description: The Table Maintenance Request Form will be the primary input document from which the personnel department will extract table update functions. The form will allow for multiple updates to one table, or multiple or single updates to many tables. The form will also allow the user to request the deletion of a table or the generation of reports.

The form will include the following fields: Clerk Code, Security Table Name, Table Key, Field Number To Be Changed, New Value To Be Assigned, Delete Table Indicator, Delete Entry Indicator, Add Entry Indicator, Add Fields, List Table Indicator, and List Directory Indicator.

Distribution: To authorized personnel system users.

Volume and Frequency: To be determined.

C.   REPORT REQUEST FORM

Purpose: To provide the user with a vehicle to request special reports from the personnel system.

Description: The Report Request Form will provide the personnel department Report Writer with enough information to generate a requested report within an appropriate time period. The content of this form will include:

- A description of the report request
- The date and time the requestors would like their output
- An indication as to whether this is a one-time report request
- An indication as to whether it will be requested on a scheduled basis (daily, weekly, monthly)
- Number of copies
- Any special notes that might assist the personnel department report writer.

The form will have to include an authorized signature which will be verified by the personnel department report writer.

Distribution: As noted on form.

Volume and Frequency: To be determined.

APPENDIX B
OUTPUTS

A. TRANSACTION CODE FILES FOR THE EXISTING PAYROLL SYSTEM

Transaction code files will be produced and passed to the payroll system on a weekly basis in conformance with the respective payroll schedules. Accordingly, appropriate deadline for submission of data to the personnel system must be established. Transaction codes will be in existing payroll formats.

B. PERSONNEL PROFILES

Where Personnel Profiles are still required, a new five-part Profile will be generated reflecting the added or reactivated individual's information. The Profile will be generated reflecting the new information as well as all the other information unchanged from the previous Profile. Any data changed will be highlighted on the new Personnel Profile. Generation of profiles will be on a weekly basis, unless user requirements dictate differently, by organization and by Individual's Last Name.

Purpose: To provide a display (visual summary) of an individual's basic personnel record as maintained by the personnel system and to serve as the primary vehicle for making changes and corrections to the information which comprises this basic record.

Description: This is a five-part turnaround document which will form the basic personnel record and contain seven major categories of information about the individual:

1. personal data
2. organizational assignment
3. employment status or personnel relationship
4. job
5. compensation
6. formal education
7. prior work experience.

The originator will cross out the information to be changed and print the new information in the space provided on the action copy.

Distribution: Two copies (the action copy and the file copy) to the individual's manager, one to the appropriate personnel functional area, and two extra copies (one for the individual's department and one for the payroll area if appropriate). A secure distribution system will be devised.

Volume and Frequency: The Personnel Profile will be produced weekly.

C. ACTION REPORTS

Multiple-part action reports displaying current and proposed job and personnel status data will be produced from the Suspense Data Base. These reports will be sorted by organization and distributed to appropriate individuals with personnel authorization and personnel functional areas. They will be in the form of turnaround documents which allow for corrections to be entered and require, when appropriate, the signature of the authorized individual. In special cases, these reports will be returned with authorization to the personnel department. There the operator calls up a screen of the proposed job data or proposed personnel status data carried in the Suspense Data Base and then enters the authorization indicator. This permits the transaction to be released automatically on its effective date (or on the input date if the effective date is retroactive) to update the master record.

1. Add or Reactivation Action Report

Purpose: To display data of individuals added to the personnel system but who are not yet due to report for work. On the report day, the report is used either to delete or process the transaction, depending on whether or not the person reported for work.

Description: The Add or Reactivation Action Report will display the following information: Individual's Name, Job Effective Date, Organizational Assignment Number, Organizational Assignment Title, Job Number, Job Title (and Job Grade where applicable). The report will provide a block for indicating whether or not the person reported for work.

Volume and Frequency: The Add or Reactivation Action Report will be produced weekly.

2. Job Action Report

Purpose: To display proposed job changes before they update the Personnel Data Base for review, correction, and appropriate authorization where required.

Description: The Job Action Report will display the following current and proposed job data: Individual's Name, Job Effective Date, Organizational Assignment Number, Organizational

Assignment Title, Job Number, Job Title (and Job Grade where applicable). The report will provide a block for the authorized signature and be designed as a two- or three-part turnaround document. It will be sorted by organization (major department), next by individual, and then by effective date and transactions (so a pending job transaction and compensation transaction would be displayed together for the same individual's name).

Distribution: One copy to the individual with personnel authority, one to the personnel functional area, and, where applicable, one to Salary Administration.

Volume and Frequency: The Job Action Report will be produced bi-weekly. The annual number of job changes is to be determined.

3. Bi-Weekly Salary Action Report

Purpose: To display current and projected compensation information for those individuals who will be receiving an increase, when authorized, on the next bi-weekly pay cycle. Modifications, additions, deletions, and authorization may be made directly on this form.

Description: The Bi-Weekly Salary Action Report will display for those individuals who are scheduled to receive a compensation increase all pertinent compensation information: Individual's Name, Compensation Effective Date, Projected Increases due to Merit Pool process, Projected Increases due to submission of Personnel Profiles, Job Grade, Seniority, Organizational Assignment, Job Number and Title, and Current Salary. The report will provide areas in which to add new information and change existing information. Additionally, the report will be designed as a turnaround document which will be sent to the personnel department, which will enter all items that have been authorized.

Distribution: Copies to operational managers, individuals with personnel authorization, and appropriate personnel functional areas.

Volume and Frequency: Bi-Weekly

4. Organizational Assignment Action Report

Purpose: To display proposed Organizational Assignment changes before they update the Personnel Data Base for review, correction, and appropriate authorization when required.

Description: The Organizational Assignment Action Report will display the following data: Individual's Name, Organizational Assignment Effective Date, Organizational Assignment Number, and Levels associated with Organizational Assignment Number.

Distribution: One copy to the individual with personnel authorization and one to the personnel functional area.

Volume and Frequency: The Organizational Assignment Action report will be produced daily if there exists a proposed Organizational Assignment change.

5. Leave Action Report

Purpose: To display proposed leaves (personal, maternity, salary continuance) before they update the Personnel Data Base for review, correction, and appropriate authorization where required.

Description: The report will display the current and proposed leave data and will provide a block for the authorized signature.

Distribution: One copy to the individual with personnel authorization and one to the personnel functional area.

Volume and Frequency: The report will be produced daily. The annual number of transactions is unknown at this time.

6. Employment Type Action Report

Purpose: To display selected hourly status employees (regular or part-time status only) who are about to obtain six months of service.

Description: The report will display the current and proposed data and will provide a block for the authorized signature.

Distribution: One copy to the individual with personnel authorization and one to the personnel functional area.

Volume and Frequency: The report will be produced daily as needed. The annual number of transactions is expected to be about 150.

D. NOTIFICATION REPORTS

The primary function of notification reports will be to appraise interface systems and areas of personnel actions that will affect them. These reports will display all data necessary to inform the area and/or individual what has been changed in the Personnel Data Base. The sequence of these outputs will be by organization and by Individual's Last Name. These outputs should provide sufficient data to enable interfacing organizations and parties with minimal data to effect changes within their respective areas of control and responsibility. These outputs will:

- Be in a sequence acceptable to using parties and
- Contain English explanations of Organizational Assignment Transactions effected.

After the master record has been changed, notification reports will be produced to inform interested parties (who do not require a copy of the updated Personnel Profile) of job or personnel status changes. The Security Update Notification Report will document that the changes requested on the personnel system Security Status Form were completed. The Notification Report will primarily be a narrative stating that security changes for Security Clerk Code Numbers have been made. There will need to be an authorized signature on the report (probably the personnel system Security Coordinator or designated representative).

E. ERROR REPORTS

Transactions can be rejected at two points: at data entry and when the transactions are processed from the Suspense Data Base to the Personnel Data Base. Error Reports will be generated on a daily basis sequenced by organization and by individual's last name.

    These outputs should be in a sequence meaningful to the respective recipient. Error messages generated should be in English and cite clearly and simply what the error is. The error output will be formatted in such a manner to allow it to be used as a turnaround document.

F. AUDIT AND CONTROL REPORT

Audit and control reports will be produced daily. These will be received, analyzed, and maintained by the personnel department. This report will display all data necessary to satisfy the guidelines of the auditing department and the needs of the personnel department, and interfacing systems relative to audit trails. Copies will go to the personnel department and interfacing systems.

G. TABLE LIST

Purpose: To provide the personnel department or the appropriate users with current hard copy listings of requested tables.

    Description: These reports will be produced each time a table has been changed. They will be formatted listings of each table and will be stored within the personnel department. Requested lists for users will be delivered to the administration group, separated, and sent to the appropriate users. The table directory can also be requested.

    The Table List will be a different report for each table. Typically they will contain all the fields on each table produced in a formatted and legible manner. The Table Data Base directory list will be a formatted list of the table of contents of the Table Data Base.

Distribution: Personnel department and appropriate users.
Volume and Frequency: As requested.

APPENDIX C
SYSTEM FLOWCHART

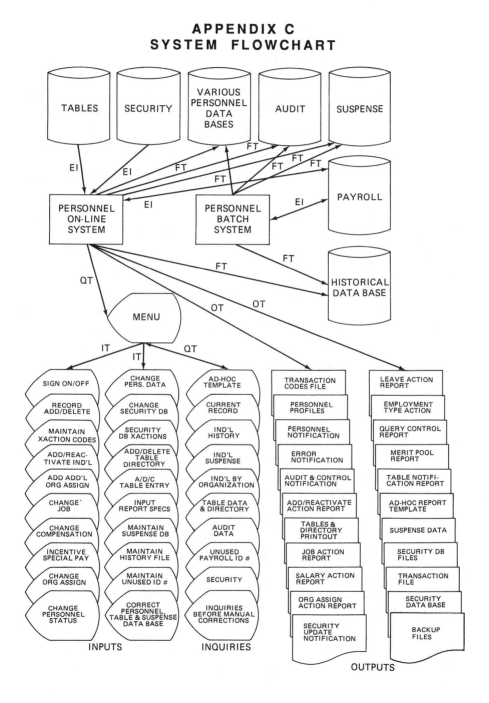

5

FPA Maintenance and Modification: Rules and On-line Parts System Example

As was mentioned previously, Function Point Analysis can also be used to size and evaluate maintenance and modification work efforts. Repair activities—exterminating bugs—only make the system do what was promised and as such do *not* produce any new value to the system; similarly, replacement of an obsolete tax table with current values provides no new benefits (in fact, it produces fewer if the tax rates have increased!) and therefore no new function points to the total. And although most enhancement requests are user-originated, *all* such requests must be user-approved. The magnitude of this effort will be seen differently by end users and data processing personnel because each group looks through opposite ends of the telescope. The end user will be interested only in the final, net change[11]

[11]Over the years, the subject of change and how to account for it has caused much debate. The issue is one of magnitude—specifically, how to credit, charge, and account for *small* changes. A change may be defined for outputs, inquiries, and inputs as *small* if and only if fewer than 20% of the data items change (in format or in processing logic) but exactly the same files are referenced or modified (not just the number). A change may be defined for files and interfaces as *small* if and only if fewer than 20% of the data items change (in format or in processing logic) but *none* of the relationships in which this file participates (or record types, if applicable) do in any way. It has been recommended (*Handbook*, Section 6) that such small changes be given half credit. This definition would even include changing field length or attributes, column position, etc.—"different format," true—but let's not cut things down to frog hairs! Local management must resolve this issue for your particular environment. My position on it is this: Unless a change is substantial enough to pay its own way, using Albrecht's indicated methodology as followed in this chapter, it should be considered to "come with the territory"—and be factored into your service-pricing table—or billed directly according to time expended and resources consumed. This would be especially appropriate for those cases in which a required enhancement changes no files, outputs, or inputs yet still requires a great deal of time to do. Moreover, the absence of such an easy-to-abuse cost overrun mechanism will *force* better, more accurate, and more complete structured analysis and design *up front*. ("Proper planning prevents poor performance!"—remember?) Finally, we can get on with things, with no loss of production arguing over milliseconds and micropoints, if we know from the start that miscellaneous nickel-and-dime items have already been accounted for and need not concern us now. We must not allow "small change" to cost us "big bucks"!

to his or her system; the net end-user modification value would be the function point sum of total business functions added less total business functions deleted, all adjusted for any changes in environmental complexity introduced. On the other hand, the data processing department will be interested in how long these modifications will take and what the total cost will be—that is, the total work required regardless of whether or not the alterations appear in the final version of the application. For MIS sizing and costing purposes, then, we need also to include system changes. They would be added to the *sum*, not the difference, of system additions and deletions. This is because it takes time and money to change or delete functions as well as to add them. As was the case with the net modification value, this sum is also adjusted for any changes in environmental complexity introduced. Also, the proper order by which to evaluate each is files and interfaces, then outputs, inquiries, and inputs.

TOTAL MODIFICATION

Let us look at these two values more closely, beginning with the *total* project size, or Development Work-Product as it is called by Albrecht. (The *net* project size is indicated by the Support Work-Product; Albrecht includes in its definition the original system value to track the total function points supported by the project during the applicable time period.) We have already seen this value in its simplest form when we filled out the on-line parts system Summary Sheet. In this case, the total system value, or size, is equal to the product of the total unadjusted function points and the production environment adjustment factor. The on-line parts system we studied earlier has a total system value, or size, of 75 function points. This value was found by multiplying the sum of all new business functions added, or 70, by the production environment adjustment factor we found to be 1.07. Since this was the first version of a new system, we had no changes or deletions, only additions. Also, we had no changes to the production environment. The on-line parts system was summarized as shown in Figure 26 (note the change in Summary Sheet format; the earlier Summary Sheet was a simplification that cannot be used when changes and deletions are introduced):

FIGURE 26. On-Line Parts System: Complete Summary Sheet.

Business Function	SIMPLE			AVERAGE			COMPLEX		
	Number	Factor	Total	No.	Factor	Total	No.	Factor	Total
1. ADDED FUNCTIONS									
OUTPUTS	2	* 4 =	8	2	* 5 =	10	0	* 7 =	0
INQUIRIES	3	* 4 =	12	0	* 5 =	0	0/0	* 6 =/*7=	0/0
INPUTS	3	* 3 =	9	0	* 4 =	0	0	* 6 =	0
FILES	3	* 7 =	21	0	* 10 =	0	0	* 15 =	0
INTERFACES	2	* 5 =	10	0	* 7 =	0	0	* 10 =	0
TOTAL ADDED: 70			60			10			0

FIGURE 26.   On-Line Parts System: Complete Summary Sheet. (continued)

Processing Complexity Factors

Factor	Value	Factor	Value
1. Data communications	3	8. On-line update	3
2. Distributed data or processing	0	9. Complex processing	1
3. Performance objectives	5	10. Code reusability	0
4. Tight configuration	5	11. Implementation/installation ease	2
5. High transaction rate	4	12. Operational ease	5
6. On-line inquiry/data entry	3	13. Multiple site installation	5
7. End user efficiency	2	14. Facilitate change	4
		TOTAL DEGREE OF INFLUENCE	42

FINAL CALCULATIONS

1. *Adjustment Factor:* $0.65 + (0.01 * 42) = 1.07$

2. *Final Function Point Count:*   70   *   1.07   =   <u> 75 </u> Function Points
   Total raw   AF
   FP count

New additions to this system would be handled in precisely the same way. However, changes and deletions cannot be handled correctly; we need to account for them as follows (do files and interfaces first, then outputs, inquiries, and inputs):

- *Changes* are combined with additions and multiplied by the resulting production environment adjustment factor;
- *Deletions* are multiplied by the production environment adjustment factor as it existed prior to project start; and
- These two sums are added together to give the total work function-point measure required. In turn, this value is then multiplied by the appropriate production delivery rate to indicate the required work effort.

More precisely, we may define the *total project size* to be:

$$[(DEL * AF_b) + (ADD + CHG_a) * AF_a]$$

where:

DEL =   unadjusted function point total deleted from the application;
AF_b =   production environment complexity adjustment (adjustment factor) pertaining to the application *before* project start;

ADD = unadjusted function point total added to the application (or tallied for a new system);

CHG_a = unadjusted function point total changed in the application and evaluated as it is expected to be at project completion ("after"); and

AF_a = production environment complexity adjustment (adjustment factor) pertaining to the application *after* project completion.

Note that we need to evaluate the expected production environment adjustment factor both before project start and after project completion. Also note that we need to list additions, deletions, and changes separately. If (and only if) AF_a = AF_b—that is, either no changes are introduced into the production environment or else they cancel each other out in the total AF count—the equation may be reduced to:

$$[(ADD + CHG_a + DEL) * AF_{a\ or\ b}\ ].$$

Our Summary Sheet for total project size will, therefore, look as shown on subsequent pages in Figure 27.

FIGURE 27. Summary Sheet—Total Modification.

SUMMARY SHEET—TOTAL MODIFICATION
APPLICATION:_____

Business Function	SIMPLE			AVERAGE			COMPLEX			Line Totals
	Number	Factor	Total	Number	Factor	Total	Number	Factor	Total	
1. ADDED FUNCTIONS										
OUTPUTS		* 4=			* 5=			* 7=		
INQUIRIES		* 4=			* 5=			* 6=/*7=		
INPUTS		* 3=			* 4=			* 6=		
FILES		* 7=			*10=			*15=		
INTERFACES		* 5=			* 7=			*10=		
TOTAL ADDED	_____			_____			_____		TOTAL	
									ADD_____	
2. "AFTER" CHANGES										
OUTPUTS		* 4=			* 5=			* 7=		
INQUIRIES		* 4=			* 5=			* 6=/*7=		
INPUTS		* 3=			* 4=			* 6=		
FILES		* 7=			*10=			*15=		
INTERFACES		* 5=			* 7=			*10=		
TOTAL "AFTER" CHANGES	_____			_____			_____		TOTAL CHG_a_____	

FIGURE 27.   Summary Sheet—Total Modification. (continued)

Business Function	SIMPLE			AVERAGE			COMPLEX			Line Totals
	Number	Factor	Total	Number	Factor	Total	Number	Factor	Total	
3. DELETED FUNCTIONS										
OUTPUTS		* 4=			* 5=			* 7=		
INQUIRIES		* 4=			* 5=			* 6=/*7=		
INPUT		* 3=			* 4=			* 6=		
FILES		* 7=			* 10=			* 15=		
INTERFACES		* 5=			* 7=			* 10=		
TOTAL DELETED		_____			_____			_____ TOTAL DEL_____		

Processing Complexity Factors

Factor	Before	After	Comments	Factor	Before	After	Comments
1. Data communications				8. On-line update			
2. Distributed data/ processing				9. Complex processing			
3. Performance objectives				10. Code reusability			
4. Tight configuration				11. Conversion/installation ease			
5. High transaction rate				12. Operational ease			
6. On-line inquiry/data entry				13. Multiple site installation			
7. End user efficiency				14. Facilitate change			

TOTAL DEGREE OF INFLUENCE DI_b_____   _____DI_a

FINAL CALCULATIONS

1. *Adjustment Factors:* (AF_b = BEFORE, AF_a = AFTER)

$$AF_b = 0.65 + (0.01 * \underline{\qquad}) = \underline{\qquad}$$
$$DI_b$$
$$AF_a = 0.65 + (0.01 * \underline{\qquad}) = \underline{\qquad}$$
$$DI_a$$

2. *Final Function Point Count,*
TOTAL Modification:

$$[\underline{\quad} * \underline{\quad}] + [(\underline{\quad} + \underline{\quad}) * \underline{\quad}] = \underline{\qquad} \text{ Function Points}$$
DEL AF_b ADD CHG_a AF_a TOTAL
                                             MODIFICATION

We have already seen how the initial version of the on-line parts system looks. We found a total of 70 raw function points and a production environment adjustment factor of 1.07, resulting in a final function point total of 75. Now let's suppose we modify the system so that the following 11 data items are added to the Parts Master File and to the Selected-Parts File:

ABC-class
date-available
date-of-last-receipt
date-of-last-sale
lot-control-flag
primary-vendor
product-group
sell-bill-unit
stock-keep-unit
stock-purchase-unit
taxable-item-flag.

The three date items and the primary-vendor item are added to the Parts Location File, raising its total number of data items to 10 (including part-number and size-code, which are common to the Parts Description File). The remaining items are added to the Parts Description File, raising its total number of data items to 12 (including part-number and size-code). The key to each file remains unchanged, no new keys are created, and no file participates in any new relationships. A total of 20 unique data items are now stored in the physical Parts Master File and in the physical Selected-Parts File. A new report, the Parts Inventory Master Report, will be provided which will list all 20 items in detail (for all stock carried) along with the date and time of report generation. This master report will be requested through the main menu. The same information, but for one stock item only, will also be provided on the Parts Inventory Display inquiry screen; the required input will remain the same.

Let us also make the following changes:

- The Selection Control Summary Report will be expanded to report on out-of-stock items that have been selected for addition to the Parts Selection Table. If an item has been selected and is currently out of stock, the report will print the part number, its description and size code, the date of the last stock order, the total number ordered, and the expected stock receipt date. If no selected parts are currently out of stock, the word "NONE" will appear next to the header "OUT OF STOCK ITEMS" on the report.
- The ability to remove a part from the Selected-Parts File is deleted (note: this is done for example purposes only; in so tight a system as this, it would be inadvisable actually to remove this ability).
- Distributors can no longer access the system.

What effects will these changes have on the on-line parts system? Remember in a planned system we evaluate outputs, inquiries, and inputs before we evaluate files and interfaces. But in a system already designed or installed, it is usually easier to evaluate changes to files and interfaces before we evaluate changes to outputs, inquiries, and inputs.

First, files and interfaces. Recall that both files and interfaces are analyzed with respect to their logical, not physical, arrangement. Were this not the case, we would count the Selected-Parts File and its interface with the Parts Master File as one average file (since there are two record formats—yet still only one relationship between them; we would select the determinant of greater complexity, or record format in this case—and 20 data items) and one average interface (for exactly the same reason) for a total of 17 (= 10 + 7) function points. However, this would *not* be correct.

As was the case before, we would count one file and one interface for each *logical* file contained in the Selected-Parts File. Since the Parts Description File now contains 12 data items and the Parts Location File now contains 10, we find both files remain simple. So do their interfaces with the Parts Master File. This modification will have no effect on either the files' or the interfaces' contribution to total function points. The new Detail Sheet entries would be as shown in Figures 28 and 29. (For easier reading, all figures (28-42) relating to this exercise have been placed together at the end of this chapter.) For easy comparison, original entries are also provided.

Because more data is being captured and stored by the on-line parts system, more information is now available for reports and inquiries. In its enhanced state, the on-line parts system will provide a completely new report, an expanded Selection Control Summary Report, and an expanded Parts Inventory Display screen.

Consider first the new Parts Inventory Master Report. This report will print the date and time of report generation plus all 20 data items distributed between the Parts Description File and the Parts Location File. These 22 data items, referenced from two logical files, give us our first complex report. Since it is a new report, it would be described on the Detail Sheet as shown in Figure 30. It would also be listed under the "Added Functions" portion of the Summary Sheet as shown in Figure 31.

Now consider the expanded Selection Control Summary Report. Because parts can no longer be removed from the Selected-Parts File, the "Parts Removed" field is no longer needed. (We shall deal with the effect on Inputs shortly.) The report will still contain all other items from the original report. To these will be added information on parts selected but currently out of stock: part number, description, size code, date of last order, total on order, and date available. Description and size-code come from the Parts Description File, the others from the Parts Location File. Recall that in the original report, one field, net change, was calculated and printed but not stored; it still added to the total data item count for complexity classification purposes. In this report addition, the current quantity on hand (total-stock-available) is stored and calculated but not printed; it is used only to determine whether or not detailed product information should be printed. But like the net change field, it too counts as one data item when classifying complexity. This enhanced Selection Control Summary Report accesses three files and 11 data items (including net change and total-stock-available) and would be classified as average. (Footnote: since parts may no longer be removed from the Selected-Parts File, only added, the net change field should, of course, equal the number of parts added to the Parts Selection Table. One could therefore argue with merit that net change, which represents the change in size of the Selected-Parts File, should not be printed at all. Rather, the number of parts added to the Parts Selection Table could— or should—provide the same information. In this case, a fourth file, the Parts Selection Table, would be accessed and the report would be rated complex. The end user must decide and approve which processing method will be used; perhaps even both fields would be wanted for comparison and internal audit purposes. If money is a factor in the decision, it is probably unlikely the extra two function points (complex = 7, average = 5) will be approved. But let the users decide this—after all, it is *their* system, not yours!)

The Detail Sheet and Summary Sheet presented in Figures 30 and 31 show how the enhanced Selection Control Summary Report would be recorded. Since this is a modified report and not a new one, we need to enter its values under the "After Changes" portion of the form, not the "Added Functions". Note that the entire report and not just its enhancements is classified. If only the enhancements were counted, the report would be classified as simple (3 - 2 = 1 file, 11 - 5 = 6 data items). It is not cheating to count the entire report (not just net value) for development purposes because this, among other reasons, compensates for the additional work we did earlier enhancing the files for no credit. Of course, there will be times that no additional outputs (or inquiries/inputs) credit may be claimed because the changes just are not big enough—again, local management must resolve this issue for your particular organization, but the law of large numbers may actually do it for you. Furthermore, this awards the points more appropriately—for providing users with more useful and timely information which they can use to manage their operations better. One should not lose sight of the human dimension in this, or any other, set of equations and technologies.

The expanded Parts Inventory Display inquiry screen is evaluated in precisely the same way as was the Parts Inventory Master Report. All 20 items from the bigger Selected-Parts File will be displayed on the screen. There is, however, no need to report date and time on an inquiry screen. The 20 items reported are still sufficient to classify this inquiry as complex. Again note that the entire inquiry and not just its enhancements is classified. If only the enhancements were counted, the inquiry would be classified as simple (2 - 2 = 0 files, 20 - 4 = 16 data items). For the same reasons we saw with outputs—fair compensation and more appropriate point awards—all the new inquiry is claimed here, not just its enhancements. We would describe this new inquiry on the Detail Sheet as shown in Figure

32. It would also be listed under the "After Changes" portion of the Summary Sheet as shown in Figure 33.

As was noted earlier, in so tight a system as this—and for practical reasons as well—we would not remove the ability to delete a part from the Selected-Parts File. We do this for example purposes only. We have already eliminated the "Parts Removed" field from the Selection Control Summary Report; this had no great effect on the enhanced report except, quite unusually, for the proper number of files to be accessed—and this small ambiguity would not even have arisen in a real-world situation. (In this case, both parts added to and removed from the Parts Selection Table would be accessed and printed, a total of four files would be referenced, and the report would clearly be classified as complex—four files, 12 data items.) For fit-and-finish purposes, the corresponding selection would also be removed from the main menu screen. The resulting Detail and Summary Sheets would appear as shown in Figures 34 and 35; note that the entry is recorded under the "Deleted Functions" portion of the form.

Combining the new report, the enhanced report, the enhanced inquiry, and the deleted input onto one Summary Sheet would give us the unadjusted total modification project size as shown in Figure 36.

Before we can complete the rest of the form, we need to see what changes, if any, will occur in the production environment complexity adjustment factor. Recall that the distributors will no longer have access to the modified on-line parts system. The only factor likely to be affected is factor 13, multiple site installation. Earlier, because three internal divisions and various distributors would help plan, review, and approve the new system, we rated the factor a 5 because of the greatly increased amount of co-ordination necessary among the different—and in the case of the distributors, diverse—work groups. Since coordination with the distributors is no longer required, we reduce factor 13, multiple site use, from 5 to 4 and leave all others as they were; this is shown in Figure 37.

Using Figures 36 and 37, we may now complete the Final Calculations portion of the Summary Sheet, as shown in Figure 38.

This value, 23 function points, would be the number used for MIS sizing, costing, and scheduling purposes. It reflects the total amount of analysis, design, programming, and testing effort required to effect the desired additions, changes, and deletions to our on-line parts system. It would be multiplied by your shop's appropriate production delivery rate to indicate the total number of hours required; this value would in turn be multiplied by your shop's appropriate (fully-burdened) labor rate to determine the total cost. This is discussed more fully in Chapter 6.

It is *not* appropriate, however, to add this value to the original function point total because both changed and deleted functions would be at least partially double-counted. So the value of this modified system is *not* 98 (= 75 + 23); we shall soon see what its correct value is. Besides being of obvious interest to data processing management for the reasons listed above, this figure will also be of interest to the end users because it will help justify the cost and time required to perform these modifications.

NET MODIFICATION

End users will also, of course, be interested in the net value of these modifications. This value may be determined from a similar form, the Net Modification Summary Sheet. The top half is precisely the same as the Total Modification Summary Sheet, but includes a section entitled "Before Changes". This section is necessary to complete the Final Calculations portion of the form. As was the case with Total Modification, the proper order by which to evaluate Net Modification is files and interfaces, then outputs, inquiries, and inputs. The complete Net Modification Summary Sheet looks as shown in Figure 39.

From this form it may be seen that the *net project size* is defined as:

$$[- (DEL + CHG_b) * AF_b + (ADD + CHG_a) * AF_a].$$

The variables in the Final Calculations portion may be defined as follows:

DEL = unadjusted function point total deleted from the application;

CHG_b = unadjusted function point total changed in the application and evaluated at project start ("before");

AF_b = production environment complexity adjustment (adjustment factor) pertaining to the application *before* project start;

ADD = unadjusted function point total added to the application;

CHG_a = unadjusted function point total changed in the application and evaluated as it is expected to be at project completion ("after"); and

AF_a = production environment complexity adjustment (adjustment factor) pertaining to the application *after* project completion.

Note that we need to evaluate both changes and the expected production environment adjustment factor both before project start and again after project completion:

- *Deletions* are combined with changes as they existed at project start. The *negative* of this sum is then multiplied by the original production environment adjustment factor;
- *Additions* are combined with changes as they are expected to be at project completion and then multiplied by the resulting production environment adjustment factor; and
- These two sums are added together to give the net work value provided. If (and only if) $AF_a = AF_b$—that is, either no changes are introduced into the

production environment or else they cancel each other out in the total AF count—the equation may be reduced to:

$$[(ADD + CHG_a) - (DEL + CHG_b)] \ [AF_{a \ or \ b}].$$

The net value, or size, of the *entire* application will be the sum of the net modification or enhancement value (in its original or simplified form, as appropriate) and the original-system total adjusted function point count. For greater accuracy, you should recalculate the original system value to at least two decimal places accuracy, and then add this value to the net modification value, calculated with similar precision, before either value is rounded. But unlike Total Modification, we do *not* multiply this figure by the production delivery rate; such a number would be meaningless and, as we shall see next, would seriously undercount by

$$[(2 * DEL + CHG_b) * AF_b] \ \text{function points}$$

the required MIS work effort.

How do these values—Total Modification and Net Modification—relate to each other? By using simple algebra, we see that these two values will *always* vary from each other as follows:

TOTAL: $(DEL * AF_b)$ + $(ADD * AF_a) + (CHG_a * AF_a)$
- NET: – $(DEL * AF_b) - (CHG_b \ * AF_b) + (ADD * AF_a) + (CHG_a * AF_a)$
_____

DIFFERENCE: $(2 * DEL * AF_b)$ $+ (CHG_b * AF_b)$
= $(2 * DEL + CHG_b) * AF_b.$

Thus,

Total Modification - $(2 * DEL + CHG_b) * AF_b$
= Net Modification, and
Net Modification + $(2 * DEL + CHG_b) * AF_b$
= Total Modification.

The only time in which Total Modification would equal Net Modification is if the application were to consist of only new or added functions—no changes or deletions. If either of these is introduced, Total Modification will always differ from Net Modification by the amount $[(2 * DEL + CHG_b) * AF_b]$.

What will be the Net Modification value of our on-line parts system? Earlier we found the Total Modification value to be 23 function points; the Net Modification value may be determined as shown in Figure 40.

This value, 8 function points, is the net total added to the modified on-line parts system—the net total additional business functions provided. But they cost almost three times that much to produce. As with so many other things, *doing it right the first time is far less expensive* (you don't really believe, do you, that you have neither time nor money to do it right the first time—but have plenty of both to fix it the second (or third, or fourth, or...) time around—*do you?*). In any case, the new system value is *83* function points (= 75 + 8), not—as mentioned earlier— 98. Does the difference between Total and Net Modification values here follow the equation we developed earlier? Yes. $(2 * 3 + 8) * 1.07 = 14.98$, which when rounded is equal to $(23 - 8)$.

Had we developed the resulting application all at one time, with no modification, we could have used the Total, the Net, or the original Summary Sheet to record our totals, as we have done in Figure 41.

If we had used the Total or Net Modification Summary Sheet, our answer would, of course, be the same; note that only the "Added Functions" and "After" factor portions of the form would be used, as shown in Figure 42.

In summary, our on-line parts system has a final value of 83 function points, although the equivalent of 98 was required to produce it.

This represents by far the most accurate, technology-independent project sizing method generally known today; in addition to its superior accuracy, Function Point Analysis provides the *only* method which can both be utilized *before* the code is written (as early as *5%* of total project duration!), and be understood and evaluated by end users before or after the program is implemented. With greater use and understanding, its accuracy is sure to improve even more. Soon new systems may be sized to within 5-10% accuracy—even before "IDENTIFICATION DIVISION.", "PROCEDURE OPTIONS (MAIN);", or other relevant first code line is ever written!

FIGURE 28.   On-Line Parts (Modified) Files—Detail.

Detail Sheet			
Application: On-line Parts (Modified)	Function Type: Files		
Description:	Simple	Average	Complex
BEFORE			
Parts Selection Table (1 relationship, 2 data items)	1		
Selected-Parts File - 2 logical files			
1. Parts Description (1 relationship, 5 data items)	1		
2. Parts Location (1 relationship, 6 data items)	1		
AFTER			
Parts Selection Table (1 relationship, 2 data items)	1		
Selected-Parts File - 2 logical files			
1. Parts Description (1 relationship, 12 data items)	1		
2. Parts Location (1 relationship, 10 data items)	1		
(NEW) *** TOTALS ***	3		

FIGURE 29.   On-Line Parts (Modified) Interfaces—Detail.

Detail Sheet

Application: On-line Parts (Modified)   Function Type: Interfaces

Description:	Simple	Average	Complex
BEFORE			
Parts Master File to Selected-Parts File - 2 logical files			
1. Parts Description (1 relationship, 5 data items)	1		
2. Parts Location (1 relationship, 6 data items)	1		
AFTER			
Parts Master File to Selected-Parts File - 2 logical files			
1. Parts Description (1 relationship, 12 data items)	1		
2. Parts Location (1 relationship, 10 data items)	1		
(NEW) *** TOTALS ***	2		

FIGURE 30.   On-Line Parts (Modified) Outputs—Detail.

Detail Sheet

Application: On-line Parts (Modified)   Function Type: Outputs

Description:	Simple	Average	Complex
BEFORE			
Parts Inventory Report - 2 reports			
1. Detail report (2 files, 10 data items)		1	
2. Summary report (1 file, 2 data items)	1		
Selection Control Report - 2 reports			
1. Detail report (3 files, 6 data items)		1	
2. Summary report (2 files, 5 data items)	1		
AFTER			
Parts Inventory Report - 2 reports			
1. Detail report (2 files, 10 data items)		1	
2. Summary report (1 file, 2 data items)	1		
Selection Control Report - 2 reports			
1. Detail report (3 files, 6 data items)		1	
2. Summary report (3 files, 11 data items) - change		1	
Parts Inventory Master Report (2 files, 22 data items) - new			1
(NEW) *** TOTALS ***	1	3	1

FIGURE 31.   On-Line Parts (Modified) Outputs—Summary.

SUMMARY SHEET - TOTAL MODIFICATION
APPLICATION: *ON-LINE PARTS (MODIFIED)*

Business Function	SIMPLE			AVERAGE			COMPLEX			Line Totals
	Number	Factor	Total	Number	Factor	Total	Number	Factor	Total	
1. ADDED FUNCTIONS										
OUTPUTS		* 4=			* 5=		1	* 7=	7	7
INQUIRIES		* 4=			* 5=			* 6=/*7=		
INPUTS		* 3=			* 4=			* 6=		
FILES		* 7=			*10=			*15=		
INTERFACES		* 5=			* 7=			*10=		
TOTAL ADDED		_____			_____				7 TOTAL ADD 7	
2. "AFTER" CHANGES										
OUTPUTS		* 4=		1	* 5=	5		* 7=		5
INQUIRIES		* 4=			* 5=			* 6=/*7=		
INPUTS		* 3=			* 4=			* 6=		
FILES		* 7=			*10=			*15=		
INTERFACES		* 5=			* 7=			*10=		
TOTAL "AFTER" CHANGES		_____			5			TOTAL CHG$_a$ 5	
3. DELETED FUNCTIONS										
OUTPUTS		* 4=			* 5=			* 7=		
INQUIRIES		* 4=			* 5=			* 6=/*7=		
INPUTS		* 3=			* 4=			* 6=		
FILES		* 7=			* 10=			* 15=		
INTERFACES		* 5=			* 7=			* 10=		
TOTAL DELETED		_____			_____			TOTAL DEL_____	

FIGURE 32.   On-Line Parts (Modified) Inquiries—Detail.

Detail Sheet

Application: On-line Parts (Modified)	Function Type: Inquiries		
Description:	Simple	Average	Complex
BEFORE			
Main Menu (0 files, 1 data item)	1		
Parts Description Display (1 file, 4 data items output)	1		
Parts Inventory Display (2 files, 4 data items output)	1		
AFTER			
Main Menu (0 files, 1 data item)	1		
Parts Description Display (1 file, 4 data items output)	1		
Parts Inventory Display (2 files, 20 data items output) - change			1
(NEW) *** TOTALS ***	2		1

FIGURE 33.   On-Line Parts (Modified) Inquiries—Summary.

SUMMARY SHEET—TOTAL MODIFICATION
APPLICATION: *ON-LINE PARTS (MODIFIED)*

Business Function	SIMPLE			AVERAGE			COMPLEX			Line Totals
	Number	Factor	Total	Number	Factor	Total	Number	Factor	Total	
1. ADDED FUNCTIONS										
OUTPUTS		* 4=			* 5=			* 7=		
INQUIRIES		* 4=			* 5=			* 6=/*7=		
INPUTS		* 3=			* 4=			* 6=		
FILES		* 7=			*10=			* 5=		
INTERFACES		* 5=			* 7=			*10=		
TOTAL ADDED			_____			_____			TOTAL ADD_____	
2. "AFTER" CHANGES										
OUTPUTS		* 4=			* 5=			* 7=		
INQUIRIES		* 4=			* 5=		0/1	* 6=/*7=	7	7
INPUTS		* 3=			* 4=			* 6=		
FILES		* 7=			*10=			*15=		
INTERFACES		* 5=			* 7=			*10=		
TOTAL "AFTER" CHANGES			_____			_____			7 TOTAL CHG$_a$ 7	
3. DELETED FUNCTIONS										
OUTPUTS		* 4=			* 5=			* 7=		
INQUIRIES		* 4=			* 5=			* 6=/*7=		
INPUTS		* 3=			* 4=			* 6=		
FILES		* 7=			* 10=			* 15=		
INTERFACES		* 5=			* 7=			* 10=		
TOTAL DELETED			_____			_____			TOTAL DEL_____	

FIGURE 34.   On-Line Parts (Modified) Inputs—Detail.

Detail Sheet

Application: On-line Parts (Modified)   Function Type: Inputs

Description:	Simple	Average	Complex
BEFORE			
Add part to Selection Table (1 file, 2 data items)	1		
Remove part from Selection Table (2 files, 4 data items)	1		
Request Parts Inventory Report (1 file, 2 data items)	1		
AFTER			
Add part to Selection Table (1 file, 2 data items)	1		
Request Parts Inventory Report (1 file, 2 data items)	1		
(NEW) *** TOTALS ***	2		

FIGURE 35. On-Line Parts (Modified) Inputs—Summary.

SUMMARY SHEET—TOTAL MODIFICATION
APPLICATION: *ON-LINE PARTS (MODIFIED)*

Business Function	SIMPLE			AVERAGE			COMPLEX			Line Totals
	Number	Factor	Total	Number	Factor	Total	Number	Factor	Total	
1. ADDED FUNCTIONS										
OUTPUTS		* 4=			* 5=			* 7=		
INQUIRIES		* 4=			* 5=			* 6=/*7=		
INPUTS		* 3=			* 4=			* 6=		
FILES		* 7=			*10=			*15=		
INTERFACES		* 5=			* 7=			*10=		
TOTAL ADDED			_____			_____			_____ TOTAL ADD_____	
2. "AFTER" CHANGES										
OUTPUTS		* 4=			* 5=			* 7=		
INQUIRIES		* 4=			* 5=			* 6=/*7=		
INPUTS		* 3=			* 4=			* 6=		
FILES		* 7=			*10=			*15=		
INTERFACES		* 5=			* 7=			*10=		
TOTAL "AFTER" CHANGES			_____			_____			_____ TOTAL CHG$_a$_____	
3. DELETED FUNCTIONS										
OUTPUTS		* 4=			* 5=			* 7=		
INQUIRIES		* 4=			* 5=			* 6=/*7=		
INPUTS	1	* 3=	3		* 4=			* 6=		3
FILES		* 7=			* 10=			* 15=		
INTERFACES		* 5=			* 7=			* 10=		
TOTAL DELETED			3			_____			_____ TOTAL DEL___3___	

FIGURE 36. On-Line Parts (Modified)—Unadjusted Total Modification.

SUMMARY SHEET—TOTAL MODIFICATION
APPLICATION: *ON-LINE PARTS (MODIFIED)*

Business Function	SIMPLE			AVERAGE			COMPLEX			Line Totals
	Number	Factor	Total	Number	Factor	Total	Number	Factor	Total	
1. ADDED FUNCTIONS										
OUTPUTS		* 4=			* 5=		1	* 7=	7	7
INQUIRIES		* 4=			* 5=			* 6=/*7=		
INPUTS		* 3=			* 4=			* 6=		
FILES		* 7=			*10=			* 15=		
INTERFACES		* 5=			* 7=			* 10=		
TOTAL ADDED			_____			_____			7 TOTAL ADD___7___	

FIGURE 36.   On-Line Parts (Modified)—Unadjusted Total Modification. (continued)

SUMMARY SHEET—TOTAL MODIFICATION
APPLICATION: *ON-LINE PARTS (MODIFIED)*

Business Function	SIMPLE			AVERAGE			COMPLEX			Line Totals
	Number	Factor	Total	Number	Factor	Total	Number	Factor	Total	
2. "AFTER" CHANGES										
OUTPUTS		* 4=		1	* 5=	5		* 7=		5
INQUIRIES		* 4=			* 5=		0/1	* 6=/*7=	7	7
INPUTS		* 3=			* 4=			* 6=		
FILES		* 7=			*10=			*15=		
INTERFACES		* 5=			* 7=			*10=		
TOTAL "AFTER" CHANGES		___				5			7	TOTAL CHGa 12
3. DELETED FUNCTIONS										
OUTPUTS		* 4=			* 5=			* 7=		
INQUIRIES		* 4=			* 5=			* 6=/*7=		
INPUTS	1	* 3=	3		* 4=			* 6=		3
FILES		* 7=			* 10=			* 15=		
INTERFACES		* 5=			* 7=			* 10=		
TOTAL DELETED		3			___					TOTAL DEL 3

FIGURE 37.   On-Line Parts (Modified) System Processing Complexity Factors.

Processing Complexity Factors

Factor	Before	After	Comments	Factor	Before	After	Comments
1. Data communications	3	3		8. On-line update	3	3	
2. Distributed data processing	0	0		9. Complex processing	1	1	
3. Performance objectives	5	5		10. Code reusability	0	0	
4. Tight configuration	5	5		11. Conversion/ installation ease	2	2	
5. High transaction rate	4	4		12. Operational ease	5	5	
6. On-line inquiry/ data entry	3	3		13. Multiple site installation	5	4	eliminate distributors
7. End user efficiency	2	2		14. Facilitate change	4	4	
TOTAL DEGREE OF INFLUENCE				DI_b	42	41	DI_a

FIGURE 38. On-Line Parts (Modified) Final Calculations.

FINAL CALCULATIONS

1. *Adjustment Factors:* $(AF_b = BEFORE, \ AF_a = AFTER)$

$$AF_b = 0.65 + (0.01 \ * \ \underline{\ 42\ }) = \underline{1.07} \qquad AF_a = 0.65 + (0.01 * \underline{\ 41\ }) = \underline{1.06}$$
$$ DI_b DI_a$$

2. *Final Function Point Count,*

TOTAL   Modification:
$$[\ \underline{3}\ * \ \underline{1.07}\ ] \ + \ [\ (\ \underline{\ 7\ } + \ \underline{12}\ )\ * \ \underline{1.06}\ ]\ = \ \underline{\ \ 23\ \ } \ \text{Function Points}$$
$$\ \ DEL \ \ \ AF_b ADD \ \ CHG_a AF_a TOTAL$$
$$ MODIFICATION$$

FIGURE 39. Summary Sheet—Net Modification.

SUMMARY SHEET—NET MODIFICATION
APPLICATION :_____

Business Function	SIMPLE			AVERAGE			COMPLEX			Line Totals
	Number	Factor	Total	Number	Factor	Total	Number	Factor	Total	
1. ADDED FUNCTIONS										
OUTPUTS		* 4=			* 5=			* 7=		
INQUIRIES		* 4=			* 5=			* 6=/*7=		
INPUTS		* 3=			* 4=			* 6=		
FILES		* 7=			*10=			*15=		
INTERFACES		* 5=			* 7=			*10=		
TOTAL ADDED		_____			_____			_____	TOTAL ADD_____	
2. "AFTER" CHANGES										
OUTPUTS		* 4=			* 5=			* 7=		
INQUIRIES		* 4=			* 5=			* 6=/*7=		
INPUTS		* 3=			* 4=			* 6=		
FILES		* 7=			* 10=			*15=		
INTERFACES		* 5=			* 7=			*10=		
TOTAL "AFTER" CHANGES		_____			_____			_____	TOTAL CHG_a_____	
3. DELETED FUNCTIONS										
OUTPUTS		* 4=			* 5=			* 7=		
INQUIRIES		* 4=			* 5=			* 6=/*7=		
INPUTS		* 3=			* 4=			* 6=		
FILES		* 7=			* 10=			* 15=		
INTERFACES		* 5=			* 7=			* 10=		
TOTAL DELETED		_____			_____			_____	TOTAL DEL_____	

FIGURE 39.   Summary Sheet—Net Modification. (continued)

SUMMARY SHEET—NET MODIFICATION
APPLICATION:_____

Business Function	SIMPLE			AVERAGE			COMPLEX			Line Totals
	Number	Factor	Total	Number	Factor	Total	Number	Factor	Total	
4. "BEFORE" CHANGES										
OUTPUTS		* 4=			* 5=			* 7=		
INQUIRIES		* 4=			* 5=			* 6=/*7=		
INPUTS		* 3=			* 4=			* 6=		
FILES		* 7=			*10=			*15=		
INTERFACES		* 5=			* 7=			*10=		
TOTAL "BEFORE" CHANGES	_____			_____			_____			TOTAL CHG$_b$____

Processing Complexity Factors

Factor	Before	After	Comments	Factor	Before	After	Comments
1. Data communications				8. On-line update			
2. Distributed data processing				9. Complex processing			
3. Performance objectives				10. Code reusability			
4. Tight configuration				11. Conversion/ installation ease			
5. High transaction rate				12. Operational ease			
6. On-line inquiry/ data entry				13. Multiple site installation			
7. End user efficiency				14. Facilitate change			
TOTAL DEGREE OF INFLUENCE				DI$_b$	_____	_____ DI$_a$	

FINAL CALCULATIONS

1. *Adjustment Factors:*   (AF$_b$ = BEFORE, AF$_a$ = AFTER)

$$AF_b = 0.65 + (0.01 * \underline{\quad}) = \underline{\quad} \qquad AF_a = 0.65 + (0.01 * \underline{\quad}) = \underline{\quad}$$
$$DI_bDI_a$$

2. *Final Function Point Count,*   (IMPORTANT: note minus sign!)

NET Modification:

$$- [(\underline{\quad} + \underline{\quad}) * \underline{\quad}] + [(\underline{\quad} + \underline{\quad}) * \underline{\quad}] = \underline{\quad} \text{ Function Points}$$
$$DEL \quad CHG_b \quad AF_b ADD \quad CHG_a \quad AF_a NET$$
$$ MODIFICATION$$

FIGURE 40. On-Line Parts (Modified)—Net Modification.

SUMMARY SHEET—NET MODIFICATION

APPLICATION: *ON-LINE PARTS (MODIFIED)*

Business Function	SIMPLE			AVERAGE			COMPLEX			Line Totals
	Number	Factor	Total	Number	Factor	Total	Number	Factor	Total	
1. ADDED FUNCTIONS										
OUTPUTS		* 4=			* 5=		1	* 7=	7	7
INQUIRIES		* 4=			* 5=			* 6=/*7=		
INPUTS		* 3=			* 4=			* 6=		
FILES		* 7=			*10=			*15=		
INTERFACES		* 5=			* 7=			*10=		
TOTAL ADDED			_____			_____			7	TOTAL ADD 7
2. "AFTER" CHANGES										
OUTPUTS		* 4=		1	* 5=	5		* 7=		5
INQUIRIES		* 4=			* 5=		0/1	* 6=/*7=	7	7
INPUTS		* 3=			* 4=			* 6=		
FILES		* 7=			*10=			*15=		
INTERFACES		* 5=			* 7=			*10=		
TOTAL "AFTER" CHANGES			_____			5			7	TOTAL CHG$_a$ 12
3. DELETED FUNCTIONS										
OUTPUTS		* 4=			* 5=			* 7=		
INQUIRIES		* 4=			* 5=			* 6=/*7=		
INPUTS	1	* 3=	3		* 4=			* 6=		3
FILES		* 7=			* 10=			* 15=		
INTERFACES		* 5=			* 7=			* 10=		
TOTAL DELETED			3			_____			_____	TOTAL DEL 3
4. "BEFORE" CHANGES										
OUTPUTS	1	* 4=	4		* 5=			* 7=		4
INQUIRIES	1	* 4=	4		* 5=			* 6=/*7=		4
INPUTS		* 3=			* 4=			* 6=		
FILES		* 7=			* 10=			* 15=		
INTERFACES		* 5=			* 7=			* 10=		
TOTAL "BEFORE" CHANGES			8			_____			_____	TOTAL CHG$_b$ 8

FIGURE 40.   On-Line Parts (Modified)—Net Modification. (continued)

Processing Complexity Factors

Factor	Before	After	Comments	Factor	Before	After	Comments
1. Data communications	3	3		8. On-line update	3	3	
2. Distributed data processing	0	0		9. Complex processing	1	1	
3. Performance objectives	5	5		10. Code reusability	0	0	
4. Tight configuration	5	5		11. Conversion/ installation ease	2	2	
5. High transaction rate	4	4		12. Operational ease	5	5	
6. On-line inquiry/ data entry	3	3		13. Multiple site installation	5	4	
7. End user efficiency	2	2		14. Facilitate change	4	4	

TOTAL DEGREE OF INFLUENCE DI_b 42   41 DI_a

FINAL CALCULATIONS

1. *Adjustment Factors:*   (AF_b = BEFORE, AF_a = AFTER)

$$AF_b = 0.65 + (0.01 * \underline{\ 42\ }) = \underline{1.07} \qquad AF_a = 0.65 + (0.01 * \underline{\ 41\ }) = \underline{1.06}$$
$$ DI_b DI_a$$

2. *Final Function Point Count,*   (IMPORTANT: note minus sign!)

NET Modification:

$$-\ [(\ \underline{3}\ +\ \underline{8}\ )\ *\ \underline{1.07}\ ]\ +\ [\ (\ \underline{7}\ +\ \underline{12}\ )\ *\ \underline{1.06}\ ]\ =\ \underline{\ 8\ }\ \text{Function Points}$$

    DEL CHG_b AF_b ADD CHG_a AF_a NET
                                                             MODIFICATION

FIGURE 41.   On-Line Parts (Enhanced) System: Complete Summary Sheet.

SUMMARY SHEET—SIMPLIFIED
APPLICATION: *ON-LINE PARTS (ENHANCED ORIGINAL)*

Business Function	Number	Complexity		Factor		Line Totals	Group Totals
OUTPUTS	1	Simple	*	4	=	4	
	3	Average	*	5	=	15	
	1	Complex	*	7	=	7	
TOTAL:	5						26

FIGURE 41.   On-Line Parts (Enhanced) System: Complete Summary Sheet.
(continued)

Business Function	Number	Complexity		Factor		Line Totals	Group Totals
INQUIRIES	2	Simple	*	4	=	8	
		Average	*	5	=		
		Complex	*	6	=		
	1	Complex	*	7	=	7	
TOTAL:	3						15
INPUTS	2	Simple	*	3	=	6	
		Average	*	4	=		
		Complex	*	6	=		
TOTAL:	2						6
FILES	3	Simple	*	7	=	21	
		Average	*	10	=		
		Complex	*	15	=		
TOTAL:	3						21
INTERFACES	2	Simple	*	5	=	10	
		Average	*	7	=		
		Complex	*	10	=		
TOTAL:	2						10

TOTAL UNADJUSTED FUNCTION POINTS: 78

Processing Complexity Factors			
Factor	Value	Factor	Value
1. Data communications	3	8. On-line update	3
2. Distributed data/processing	0	9. Complex processing	1
3. Performance objectives	5	10. Code reusability	0
4. Tight configuration	5	11. Conversion/installation ease	2
5. High transaction rate	4	12. Operational ease	5
6. On-line inquiry/data entry	3	13. Multiple site installation	4
7. End user efficiency	2	14. Facilitate change	4
		TOTAL DEGREE OF INFLUENCE	41

FIGURE 41.   On-Line Parts (Enhanced) System: Complete Summary Sheet.
(continued)

FINAL CALCULATIONS

1. *Adjustment Factor:* $0.65 + (0.01 * 41) = 1.06$

2. *Final Function Point Count:*   78 * 1.06 = $\underline{\text{ 83 }}$ Function Points

                                 Total raw   AF

                                 FP count

FIGURE 42.   On-Line Parts (Enhanced)—Total Modification.

SUMMARY SHEET—TOTAL MODIFICATION
APPLICATION: *ON-LINE PARTS ENHANCED ORIGINAL*

Business Function	SIMPLE			AVERAGE			COMPLEX			Line Totals
	Number	Factor	Total	Number	Factor	Total	Number	Factor	Total	
1. ADDED FUNCTIONS										
OUTPUTS	1	* 4 =	4	3	* 5=	15	1	* 7=	7	26
INQUIRIES	2	* 4 =	8		* 5=		1	* 6=/*7=	7	15
INPUTS	2	* 3 =	6		* 4=			* 6=		6
FILES	3	* 7 =	21		*10=			*15=		21
INTERFACES	2	* 5 =	10		* 7=			*10=		10
TOTAL ADDED			49			15			14	TOTAL ADD 78

Processing Complexity Factors			
Factor	Value	Factor	Value
1. Data communications	3	8. On-line update	3
2. Distributed data or processing	0	9. Complex processing	1
3. Performance objectives	5	10. Code reusability	0
4. Tight configuration	5	11. Implementation/installation ease	2
5. High transaction rate	4	12. Operational ease	5
6. On-line inquiry/data entry	3	13. Multiple site installation	4
7. End user efficiency	2	14. Facilitate change	4
TOTAL DEGREE OF INFLUENCE		DI_b____ ____41____ DI_a	

FIGURE 42. On-Line Parts (Enhanced)—Total Modification. (continued)

FINAL CALCULATIONS

1. *Adjustment Factors:* $(AF_b = BEFORE, \; AF_a = AFTER)$

$AF_b = 0.65 + (0.01 * \underline{\qquad}) = \underline{\qquad}$ $\quad$ $AF_a = 0.65 + (0.01 * \underline{\;41\;}) = \underline{1.06}$
$\; DI_b$ $\; DI_a$

2. *Final Function Point Count,*

TOTAL Modification:

$[\underline{\qquad} \; * \; \underline{\qquad}] \; + \; [(\; \underline{78} + \underline{0}\;) \; * \; \underline{1.06} \;] \; = \; \underline{\;83\;}$ Function Points
$\;\; DEL \qquad AF_b \qquad\quad ADD \;\; CHG_a \quad AF_a \qquad\qquad\qquad TOTAL$
$\qquad\qquad\qquad\qquad\qquad\qquad\qquad\qquad\qquad\qquad\qquad\qquad MODIFICATION$

6

FPA in Productivity Evaluation, Forecasting, and Cost-Benefit Analyses; Remaining Challenges

Of itself, Function Point Analysis is a project sizing technique —the very best there is—and you may at this point be wondering how big our 83-point system is. No precise definitions exist, but Unisys suggests a small system to be less than 300 function points, a medium system to be 300-800, a large system to be 800-1000, and a very large system to be greater than 1000 function points. These qualitative labels are not important; the quantitative values are. Function Point Analysis is the *only accurate* sizing technique available for use before coding even begins, and its proven accuracy of ± 15-20%—certain to improve even more (hopefully at least in part due to this book!)—runs rings and circles around other methods which after 35 years have not even standardized their definitions or methods—what *is* one line of source code, anyway?!!! (Read the next paragraph to get even more confused about this issue!)

Function Point Analysis may be used most effectively when its precision in project sizing—long the weakest component in software engineering project management techniques—is applied *directly* in time requirements forecasting, programmer productivity/quality evaluation, cost-benefit analysis, and the like. The most common way in which Function Point Analysis has been *misused* is using (actually, abusing) it to try to estimate source lines of code, from which the forecast, evaluation, or analysis is *then made*. This misuse of FPA is just plain *WRONG*! If industry cannot even decide how to define one line of code once it is written (one researcher found a huge *2300%* variance in productivity due *only* to extremely wide variations in 7 SLOC definitions!), how can FPA possibly predict it before it is written? Moreover, this two-step process introduces two levels of error into the solution, the more serious of which is the ± 50% (on average) distortion introduced when attempting to predict the number of COBOL source lines—due in large part to wide variations in programmer efficiency. So for *general reference purposes only*, you may estimate on average 100 to 120 lines of COBOL code (or 60-65 lines of PL/1 code) for each function point produced. Efficient COBOL programmers and systems generators, however, require as few as 59 lines of code to produce one function point, and inefficient programmers require substantially more than the 100 to 120 lines average. (As we shall see, efficient fourth generation language (4GL) programmers require only 14 lines of 4GL code—such as the state-of-the-art Unisys (formerly Burroughs) LINC II, or, in the DEC VAX/VMS environment, National Information Systems (San Jose, California) ACCENT R—to produce one function point that is part of a *complete system*, including normalized relational data base and message handling routines, *not* just reports and inquiries!) This again emphasizes the fact that FPA should be used directly; using source lines of code—no matter how derived and for whatever reason (usually, because they are "familiar")—is a serious and dangerous mistake which should no longer be made now that better, safer methods are available and so easily learned and applied.

It is by such direct application that Function Point Analysis can—when used with other measures—most readily and accurately forecast, evaluate, or analyze the other critical issues mentioned earlier. Local management *must* determine and use proper productivity values for its own staff and production environment—no exceptions! (It may be helpful to begin with general, average values presented here and then to modify these as you gain experience and develop an historical base which may then be used—and further refined—on future projects. Be sure to account for all major contributing factors in this analysis, such as installation of a new productivity tool or completion of training.) Otherwise, unnecessary but avoidable errors will be introduced and probably be blamed on the Function Point Analysis method instead of improper data capture and evaluation techniques, whether by omission or commission. From extensive work with AT&T productivity evaluation methods, the author knows well the various problems associated with this critical process—not the least of which is resistance by people to a new and more accurate evaluation method on which they can no longer blame poor evaluations due to high error margins. But this is actually a benefit to them and should be sold as such: Now management will know better just how long a project really *should* take! Besides thoroughly learning and properly applying the Function Point Analysis sizing technique, local management must also develop and use correct productivity evaluation measures, particularly precise time measurements. (For starting-estimate purposes *only*, AT&T and Unisys suggest you assume about 75% of the total claimed time to be spent directly on project production; the balance goes to breaks, meetings, training, overhead, and the like.) Error rates still in excess of 10-20% (at the very most) must be attributed to these measurements, not FPA, and refinements in management techniques must occur within these areas, again not Function Point Analysis.

Precisely how to do this is the subject of much current research and debate, and is beyond the scope of this book. (Interested readers are invited to study the works of James Martin, T. C. Jones (see in particular Measuring Software, forthcoming in 1989), and others for further detail.) As examples only, however, of further uses to which Function Point Analysis can (with other measures) be put, summaries of several other research efforts will be provided; details of application size, nature, environment, and other characteristics are not included. Precision in result is ensured, however, by the accuracy in the Function Point Analysis method—something simply not possible with such trouble-maker methods as counting source lines of code—again, whatever they may be! The productivity figures provided are for general guideline purposes only; for maximum accuracy, you must determine and use proper values for your particular environment. Estimates of time and money requirements depend every bit as much on these figures as they do on the project size.

Let us look first at some general productivity guidelines. Just as programmer efficiency varies widely, so does programmer (both individual and shop) productivity. Four well-known studies have estimated one COBOL function point to require anywhere from 8 to 50 hours on average to code—usually around 20; the range was from 3 to 87 hours per function point (there are programmers and shops less productive than this, but they not surprisingly avoid measurement). Local management must, of course, determine and use proper values for its own staff. By contrast, an efficient COBOL (or other language; ACCENT R is written in C and programmed in questions-and-forms driven ACCENT R, then produces expanded ACCENT R code which is itself both customizable and re-compilable for optimal fit!) systems generator requires only one hour to code one function point.

Productivity varies not only by programmer, but also by project size. Because of increasing complexity and the need for additional planning and coordination, required COBOL or PL/1 programming time for *all* function points increases approximately 2% (one researcher found 4%) with *each additional* function point! (For very large projects, this relationship changes to a *curvilinear* one increasing exponentially.) For example, the (average) programmer who requires 20 hours to program one function point in a 400-point system would require 52 hours to program one function point in a 2000-point system. The 400-point system would require 8000 hours (= 20 hrs/FP * 400 FP) to program, and the 2000-point system would require 104,000 hours (= 52 hrs/FP * 2000 FP, or, alternatively, [20 hrs/FP + (2000 FP - 400 FP) * 1.2 minutes/FP/FP ÷ 60 min/hr] * 2000 FP).

These values may be summarized in the chart shown in Figure 43 and in the following table (Source: Professor Eberhard E. Rudolph, University of Auckland, and Unisys LINC Application Support Center, Atlanta, Georgia).

PRODUCTIVITY: HOURS/FP			CODE SIZE: SLOC/FP	
	COBOL	LINC	COBOL	LINC
Average	20[*]	1[**]	100-120	14
Best	3.5	.53	59 (LINC-generated)	N/A
Worst	85.5	1.38	?	N/A

[*]plus approximately 1.2 minutes for *each additional* function point above 400

[**]essentially flat response

National Information Systems' ACCENT R produces similar productivity values.

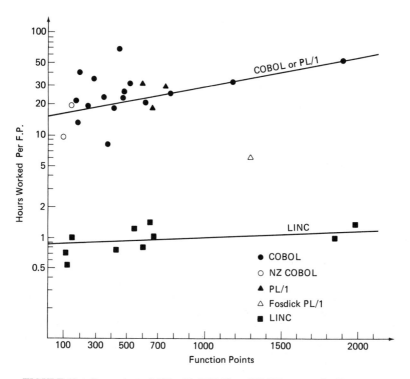

FIGURE 43.   Comparison of 4GL with COBOL and PL/1 Programming Productivity.

Figure 44 provides the *average* number of source code lines (subject to variances of productivity levels, environmental productivity tools installed and used, application size, and other factors) required to produce one function point in any of 30 languages.

FIGURE 44.   Lines-of-Code to Function Point Translation Table.
The 30 languages listed here together represent about 95% of the
world's application software; COBOL alone represents 50%. In general,
the remaining 220 or so computer languages populate the
less productive portions of this table.

Language	Level*	Average Source Lines per Function Point
1. Basic Assembler	1	320
2. Macro Assembler	1.5	213
3. C	2.5	128
4. ALGOL	3	105
5. COBOL	3	105
6. FORTRAN	3	105
7. JOVIAL	3	105
8. Mixed languages (default)	3	105
9. Other languages (default)	3	105
10. Pascal	3.5	91
11. RPG	4	80
12. MODULA-2	4.5	80
13. PL/1	4.5	80
14. Ada	4.5	71
15. BASIC	5	64
16. FORTH	5	64
17. LISP	5	64
18. PROLOG	5	64
19. LOGO	5.5	58
20. English-based languages	6	53
21. Data base languages	8	40
22. Decision support languages	9	35
23. APL	10	32
24. Statistical languages	10	32
25. OBJECTIVE-C	12	27
26. SMALLTALK	15	21
27. Menu-driven generators	20	16
28. Data base query languages	25	13
29. Spreadsheet languages	50	6
30. Graphic icon languages	75	4

*This column provides the *average number* of basic assembler source lines of code for each source line in this particular language. Although these values are both average and rounded, note the lack of precise and reliable correlation between these and average source lines per function point—again emphasizing the wisdom of employing function points *directly* and not even fooling around with code lines (whatever they may be!). Source: *SPQR/20 User Guide*, Software Productivity Research, Inc. (T.C. Jones, President), Cambridge, Massachusetts.

As can be seen, a valid *productivity* index (both development and maintenance/ defect correction, though appropriate values for each will be *different*) is *net* work hours per function point— fewer hours represents greater productivity— whereas a valid *time estimator* is gross work hours per function point (as indicated earlier, one gross work hour equals approximately 1 1/3 net work hours, so the time estimates we just calculated would for *scheduling* purposes each have to be raised by a factor of 33% —to 10,667 hours and 138,667 hours, respectively; local management must again, of course, determine and use proper values for its own staff). On the other hand, a useful programmer *quality index* is the number of program defects per function point. Fewer is, of course, better. Regardless of who caused the bug—programmer, analyst, or user—these defects require a disproportionately high amount of time and effort to identify and correct than to have done things correctly the first time.

Once programmer productivity evaluations have been accurately made, project time, money costs, and benefits may also be determined with FPA results. This is how the third category of benefits (1—project size and value; 2—programmer productivity) may be provided by Function Point Analysis—by combining the first two.

If your MIS shop is progressive, you installed a 4GL several years ago. Some shops, unfortunately, have not (but should!). Without Function Point Analysis, such a determination could not be readily made because neither project size nor development time could be accurately estimated. With FPA, however, project size may be combined with locally-determined production rates to forecast the project completion schedule. Monetary benefits resulting from earlier project completion may then be compared with costs of 4GL implementation—compiler, possibly training—to determine the net monetary benefit provided, all adjusted to reflect the time value of money.

Suppose we have the hypothetical (but with typical financials experience) XYZ Distribution Corporation.[12] Currently a manual operation, the company is trying to determine whether it should develop the following systems in a 3GL like COBOL or in a 4GL like LINC II or ACCENT R:

- General Ledger
- Order Entry
- Inventory Control
- Purchase Orders
- Sales Analysis and Forecasting.

Besides the standard "better information faster" objective, intended benefits from these systems include:

- improved cash flow
- lower inventory levels
- increased customer service levels
- greater sales
- reduced staffing requirements (development and maintenance)
- greater market share.

[12]Courtesy of: Carol Kaniper McClain, Unisys Corporation. Thanks also to Access Technology (South Natick, Massachusetts) "20/20", electronic spreadsheet of unsurpassed quality.

Four-year Pro-Forma Income Statements for a continuing manual operation may be summarized as follows:

XYZ Distribution Corporation
1986-1989 Income Projection
Fiscal Year: Calendar

	1986	1987	1988	1989
Revenue (30% growth rate)	$30,000,000	$39,000,000	$50,700,000	65,910,000
COGS (1/3 of revenue)	10,000,000	13,000,000	16,900,000	21,970,000
Margin	$20,000,000	$26,000,000	$33,800,000	$43,940,000
Expenses (80% of margin)	16,000,0000	20,800,000	27,040,000	35,152,000
Net Income Before Taxes	$4,000,000	$5,200,000	$6,760,000	$8,788,000
Taxes (estimate 50%)	2,000,000	2,600,000	3,380,000	4,394,000
Net Income	$2,000,000	$2,600,000	$3,380,000	$4,394,000

XYZ Distribution Corporation
Average DP Spending as a Percentage of Revenue
1986-1989 Projections

	1986	1987	1988	1989
Revenue	$30,000,000	$39,000,000	$50,700,000	$65,910,000
Average Industry Percentage	1.98%	1.98%	1.98%	1.98%
Average DP Expenditure	$594,000	$772,200	$1,003,860	$1,305,018
Projected DP Expenditures	-0-	-0-	-0-	-0-

Using Function Point Analysis allows us to estimate the following 3GL development times to within 15-20% accuracy (as compared with up to 200% or more error using other methods); for simplicity, however, project start and completion dates are only at the beginnings of months:

XYZ Distribution Corporation
Application Plan Schedule
Traditional 3GL Development Methodology (Mythology?)

	START DATE	COMPLETION DATE	# MONTHS AFTER IMPLEMENTATION UNTIL BENEFITS REALIZED
General Accounting	6/1/86	12/1/86	One month
Order Entry	12/1/86	6/1/87	One month
Inventory Control	10/1/86	2/1/87	One month
Purchasing	12/1/87	6/1/88	One month
Sales Forecasting	12/1/87	3/1/88	Three months

Similarly, using Function Point Analysis allows us to evaluate the 4GL development timeframe with exactly the same precision. Assumed productivity differentials in this example are extremely conservative. A good systems generator such as Unisys' LINC II or National Information Systems' ACCENT R will reduce development time to only 5% that required for COBOL—not 67% (33% for Sales Forecasting) as assumed here; this will in turn produce financial benefits (like increased revenue, decreased expenses, etc.) *20 TIMES FASTER* than the *same* system could provide if written in 3GL!!!

XYZ Distribution Corporation
Application Plan Schedule
4GL Development

	START DATE	COMPLETION DATE	# MONTHS AFTER IMPLEMENTATION UNTIL BENEFITS REALIZED
General Accounting	6/1/86	10/1/86	One month
Order Entry	6/1/86	10/1/86	One month
Inventory Control	10/1/86	2/1/87	One month
Purchasing	10/1/86	2/1/87	One month
Sales Forecasting	10/1/86	11/1/86	Three months

Benefits mentioned earlier may now be quantified and timed as follows. First we use 3GL:

XYZ Distribution Corporation
Benefit Quantification
Traditional 3GL Development Methodology

	1986	*1987*	*1988*	*1989*
REVENUE				
Order Entry				
• Reduction in revenue loss from late orders (6% to 2%)		$780,000	$2,028,000	$2,636,400
Sales Forecasting				
• Increased target account penetration (30% growth to 32% growth)			$507,000	$1,318,200
• Reduction in sales discounts (8% of revenue to 6% of revenue)			$507,000	$1,318,200
COGS				
Inventory Control				
• Reduction in spoilage (15% of COGS to 5%)			$(1,690,000)	$(2,197,000)
Purchasing				
• Increase in purchase discounts (3% of COGS)			$(253,500)	$(659,100)
Order Entry and Sales Forecasting				
• Increased COGS from increased sales (1/3 * Rev = COGS per increased unit sold + 3% discount)		$252,200	$819,650	$1,278,654
EXPENSES				
All Applications				
• Reduction in personnel	$(200,000)	$(300,000)	$(450,000)	$(600,000)
• DP capital expenditure (assumes 3rd party lease)	$40,000	$75,000	$100,000	$150,000
• DP staff	$200,000	$300,000	$400,000	$500,000
TAXES				
General Accounting				
• Tax penalty reduction (effective tax rate 45%)				
• DP capital expenditure investment tax credit (assumed by 3rd party lease)				

Next we use 4GL:

XYZ Distribution Corporation
Benefit Quantification
4GL Development

	1986	*1987*	*1988*	*1989*
REVENUE				
Order Entry	$200,000	$1,560,000	$2,028,000	$2,636,400
Sales Forecasting				
• Account penetration		$715,000	$1,014,000	$1,318,200
• Discount reduction		$715,000	$1,014,000	$1,318,200
COGS				
Inventory Control		$(1,083,333)	$(1,690,000)	$(2,197,000)
Purchasing		$325,000	$(507,000)	$(659,100)
Order Entry and Sales Forecasting	$66,666	$735,583	$983,580	$1,278,654
EXPENSES				
All Applications				
• Personnel reduction	$(200,000)	$(350,000)	$(500,000)	$(600,000)
• DP capital expenditure	$50,000	$100,000	$150,000	$160,000
• DP staff	$200,000	$300,000	$300,000	$300,000
TAXES				
General Accounting (effective tax rate 45%)				

The resulting four-year Pro-Forma Income Statements for 3GL development may be summarized as shown on the following page.

XYZ Distribution Corporation
1986-1989 Income Projection
Traditional 3GL Development Methodology

	1986	1987	1988	1989
Revenue	$30,000,000	$39,780,000	$53,742,000	$71,182,800
COGS	10,000,000	13,252,200	15,776,150	20,392,554
Margin	$20,000,000	$26,527,800	$37,965,850	$50,790,246
Expenses	16,040,000	20,875,000	27,090,000	35,202,000
Net Income Before Taxes	$ 3,960,000	$ 5,652,800	$10,875,850	$15,588,246
Taxes	1,782,000	2,543,760	4,894,133	7,014,711
Net Income	$ 2,178,000	$ 3,109,040	$ 5,981,718	$ 8,573,536
	========	========	========	========
Net Change From Current Manual Operations	$ 178,000	$ 509,040	$ 2,601,718	$ 4,179,536

XYZ Distribution Corporation
Average DP Spending as a Percentage of Revenue
1986-1989 Projections (3GL)

	1986	1987	1988	1989
Average Industry DP Expenditure (1.98%)	$ 594,000	$ 787,644	$1,064,092	$ 1,409,419
Projected DP Expenditure	$ 240,000	$ 375,000	$ 500,000	$ 650,000

    The resulting four-year Pro-Forma Income Statements for 4GL development may be summarized as shown on the following page.

XYZ Distribution Corporation
1986-1989 Income Projection
4GL Development

	1986	1987	1988	1989
Revenue	$30,200,000	$42,705,000	$54,756,000	$71,182,800
COGS	10,066,666	12,327,250	15,686,580	20,392,554
Margin	$20,133,334	$30,377,000	$39,069,420	$50,790,246
Expenses	16,050,000	20,850,000	26,990,000	35,012,000
Net Income Before Taxes	$ 4,083,334	$ 9,527,750	$12,079,420	$15,778,246
Taxes	1,837,500	4,287,488	5,435,739	7,100,211
Net Income	$ 2,245,834	$ 5,240,262	$ 6,643,681	$ 8,678,035
	=========	=========	=========	=========
Net Change from No Automation— note substantially increasing values each year.	$ 245,834	$ 2,640,262	$3,263,681	$ 4,284,035
Net Change From Traditional 3GL Development— note huge full-production 4GL advantages over 3GL in 1987 and 1988.	$ 67,834	$ 2,131,222	$ 661,963	$ 104,499

XYZ Distribution Corporation
Average DP Spending as a Percentage of Revenue
1986-1989 Projections (4GL)

	1986	1987	1988	1989
Average Industry DP Expenditure (1.98%)	$ 597,960	$ 845,559	$ 1,084,169	$ 1,409,419
Projected DP Expenditure	$ 250,000	$ 400,000	$ 450,000	$ 460,000

At first glance, nothing seems really new or different about all this—after all, both accounting and accountants have been with us for many years now. And the only thing really exciting (unless XYZ's income were *my* income!) is the overwhelming advantages achieved by earlier implementation of 4GL systems over 3GL—but progressive MIS shops have for many moons known this to be true, too. What is different—*refreshingly* different—is the underlying precision by which project development times—thus benefit realization times—may be estimated. This is one more example of the many uses to which Function Point Analysis can be applied. Another would be to evaluate the feasibility of 4GL in-house development as compared with pre-written software requiring modifications (3GL or 4GL) to achieve a proper fit to meet your business needs. Still another would be to evaluate the feasibility of cleaning up all your "spaghetti-bowl" COBOL code with optimized, structured 4GL code—then mowing down your applications backlog (before it mows you down!). How else can FPA benefit *your* MIS objectives?

Six chapters ago, we began by saying that "one of the most difficult aspects of a systems analyst's job has been the accurate estimation of project sizing, required development time, and end-user value"—a problem we immediately afterward saw was one of the "five fundamental issues that must be resolved" to satisfy some serious concerns which senior executives have "about the cost-effectiveness of their data processing departments."

ONE DOWN, FOUR TO GO! ("Mr. Albrecht, can you help us?")

We have learned how a marvelous tool—Function Point Analysis—can be used to solve not only this, but many other problems as well—both today and tomorrow! We have seen that with proper use it can—and will—every day provide levels of usefulness and precision until recently only dreamed about. But yesterday's dream is today's reality. Anyone whose life is affected by a computer processing business information—EDP/MIS staff, end user, and above all, you the valued business customer—should say, *"THANKS, AL!"*. Still, although T.C. Jones calls Function Point Analysis "the most effective software metric yet developed" (it *far* outdistances any other!), we must recognize that even it is not 100% complete or perfect. No measurement program is, ever was, or ever will be. Continuing research, discussion, and refinement efforts by Albrecht, the International Function Point User Group (Darlene Brown, President), and others will assure dynamism and the continued ability to solve the needs it so well addresses—both today *and tomorrow*! Jones, for instance, is conducting extensive research into the application of function points to real-time, operating system, aircraft navigation, avionics, and other similar software, which constitutes about 48% of all installed software; by redefining definitions and parameters, reducing internal file weights, and introducing a sixth business function group—algorithms—he is well on his way toward successful definition of a methodology he calls Feature Point Analysis! He and his consulting group also continue to research software metrics and job costing, results of which will be published in his forthcoming book <u>Measuring Software</u>.

Jones also presents this challenge to industry and researchers: to design, produce, and maintain a formal national data base of validated software productivity data that would use standard metrics (including function points), a standard chart of accounts for cost capture and reporting, and a standard set of environmental and tool descriptors, all organized by industry along Standard Industry Classification (SIC) lines. To ensure reasonable statistical accuracy, a *minimum* of 10,000 projects would be required. Interested researchers and enterprises should contact Software Productivity Research, Inc., in Cambridge, Massachusetts (1972 Massachusetts Avenue, Cambridge 02238, phone 617-495-0120).

But the main source of error in Function Point Analysis, particularly in early development stages, is incomplete or inaccurate specifications and oversight by the counter, *NOT* the FPA methodology itself! There will be those, of course, who insist on 100% accuracy and perfect proof—but while Rome burned, and their organization suffocated from "information hypoxia," they fiddled. And fiddled. And fiddled. All while awaiting the perfect proof of the perfect methodology. Far from being visionary, these people are not even on-line with the present, much less the future! "Always be sure you're right," said Lincoln, "then go ahead." With Function Point Analysis, we *are* right. We *must* go ahead. There's no choice. If we fail to plan, we must plan to fail!

The question is not whether we can afford to implement FPA.

The question is whether we can afford *not* to...

AFTERWORD

Implementing Function Point Analysis In Your Organization

Contributed by Brenda Dorr, Bank of Nova Scotia, Toronto
Edited by Ken Zwanzig (late of Grenier, St-Pierre, et Associés, Montréal) and this author
Reprinted by permission of GUIDE International

Strategically, implementing a measurement program within an organization must begin with the objectives. The starting point is high-level management, who must approve and *support* the program if it is to succeed.

Prior to the start of any training in Function Point Analysis, the entire organization must understand the whys and wherefores of a measurement program. This is achieved through a series of short presentations (with discussion) similar to the one included in this section.

Each session must be introduced by a member of senior management to demonstrate top management support for the program and to request staff commitment. Sessions should start with higher management, then middle management, and so on until all project staff have attended the overview.

The following transparencies and discussion will provide a starting point for your own introductory presentation.

MEASUREMENT OVERVIEW

- Why measure?
- What do we measure?

CONSIDERATIONS

- What do you get?
- What do we need from you?

Transparency 1

General Widgets is committed to a measurement program, which probably raises a few questions in your minds. We are going to answer those questions during the next half hour and during the discussions that follow.

Transparency 1. The answer to the question, "Why measure?" lies in the benefits to the Application Development and Maintenance (AD/M) department and the benefits to the corporation. "Throughout the history of science, progress and discoveries have been closely coupled with improvements in measurement...[These] provided the accurate information that researchers need to derive fundamental laws. Software was handicapped for more than 35 years by the very lack of accurate measurements. The traditional "lines of code" measures were not only difficult to apply, but ambiguous and paradoxical even when applied carefully. An entire generation of software researchers assumed incorrectly that improving productivity meant increasing the number of lines that could be developed per year, hence lowering the cost per source line."—T. Capers Jones. We are not going to be measuring how far it is to the coffee machine, but we will be measuring all of the aspects, etc. of AD/M that contribute to the benefits we are looking for.

This is not a one-way street by any means. Middle management and technical project staff get benefits from the results of the measurement program as we find easier ways to get the same job done. And, of course, it is your dedicated participation in meeting your professional responsibilities for this program and our company which will make it all work.

WHY MEASURE?

- Measurement and *Estimation*
- Measurement and *Improvement*
- Measurement and *Project Control*

Transparency 2

Transparency 2. The most important question about the introduction of a measurement program is, "Why measure?". The primary objective may be to improve the quality and accuracy of the cost-estimating process. This, of course, means that the past and the present must be measured in order to predict the future.

In addition to (or perhaps instead of) cost estimating, the primary objective of measurement may be productivity improvement. Measurement is needed to identify the "good things" that improve productivity (and perhaps even to "catch people doing something *right*"!—JBD), as well as areas and techniques to avoid because of their negative effect on productivity. To oversimplify for a moment, project control is primarily a question of knowing where you are—which means *measuring* where you are and comparing that with measurements of other projects of known results. Never do anything about a problem until you can make sure it exists, measure it, and quantify it.

MEASUREMENT AND ESTIMATION

Are estimating techniques effective?

How can we support estimating?

- Measure completed projects
- Build a base for future estimates
- Refine estimation and validation

Transparency 3

Transparency 3. Many organizations still rely on "experts" who can provide good estimates based on intuitive, experiential, semi-quantitative techniques (otherwise known as "gut feeling").

If right—this process cannot be taught to others. If wrong—who needs it? Many of the estimates produced vary greatly from the actual work effort for the completed project. To be blunt, many of these kinds of estimates are *WRONG*! R-squared is low, residuals are high.

Measurement can support the estimating effort. By measuring completed projects, an historical base will be created that may be used for estimating future projects. The evaluation of any variances or discrepancies which occur between the estimates and the actuals may show that the original base should be refined, or that the variation in work effort is accompanied by a variation in the work product measured between the estimate and implementation stages. Either conclusion will provide meaningful evidence to ensure that management understands the project work effort discrepancy and is assured that any necessary refinements will be made to improve the validation process.

MEASUREMENT AND IMPROVEMENT

Why do we need to improve?

Are we improving?

What can we achieve by improvement?

- Better systems developed
- Maintenance effort reduced

- More development effort
- Job satisfaction increased
- User satisfaction increased

Transparency 4

Transparency 4. Data processing installations are currently using many tools and techniques which were purchased because they promised productivity improvement. These tools and techniques appeared to be "the answer" to "the problem." The problem was thought to be the large backlog of user requirements.

The backlog still exists and may have even gotten bigger! If the promised productivity improvement is not obvious to the AD/M technical staff, what must their management or the users think about the promises?

At a minimum, we want to fix this embarrassing situation. Therefore, it is important to establish a method of measuring current productivity and future productivity to show *change over time.* This will help answer the question, "Did we get the productivity improvement we promised (or were promised)?".

It is important to note that the productivity improvement efforts are not aimed at making people do the same things faster, but are aimed at providing new tools and techniques which improve the process of building and maintaining applications, including the elimination of roadblocks and the reduction of obstacles.

What do we expect to achieve with all this improvement? With combinations of better cost estimating and better project control, we can avoid some of that last-minute (last-month?) rush to get the system done. This, combined with some realistic quality measures, will ensure that better systems are developed.

Better-quality systems will require less maintenance effort. Naturally, the "extra" time available (which translates to "recovery of lost progress") will be used to increase new application development.

We shall stop short of promising that the Garden of Eden is just around the corner, but just think a bit about what happens to staff morale and user satisfaction if more new applications and functionality are delivered, while at the same time, deadline pressure and forced overtime become an occasional event instead of a way of life.

MEASUREMENT AND PROJECT CONTROL

Evaluate work product measure
Measures do not change (except...)
Evaluation of exceptions

Transparency 5

Transparency 5. Measurement has a strong role to play in project control. The size of the project (in Function Points, for example) is a kind of definition of project scope. We shall evaluate this work product measure at various stages of the project; and, in an ideal world, this measure will not change from the beginning to the end of the project. Of course, the world and projects are not ideal. There is a lot to be learned by evaluating the exceptions.

EVALUATE WORK PRODUCT AT MILESTONES:

1. Requirements defined (5% mark)
2. General Design completed (80% mark)
3. Production application installed (100% mark)

... and other times as appropriate

Transparency 6

Transparency 6. At a minimum, the work product measure must be evaluated at three milestones in the development project. First, the project should be measured as soon as the requirements have been well identified. This is the early estimating stage, similar to the first contract of what the system must do, and occurs only about 5% into project duration.

When the general design has been completed, at about 80% into project duration, the project or system is again measured. This will be used both to control (it has grown!) and to reproject the cost estimate.

Finally (with great relief and much celebration!), the production application is installed. Measurement at this time will be used both for productivity measurement and again to identify changes and variances.

MEASURES SHOULD BE THE SAME EXCEPT FOR:

1. Approved functional changes
2. Perception of functions changed

Transparency 7

Transparency 7. If no changes in the business requirements have occurred, these measures will be the same. Any discrepancies are the result of two kinds of changes. These are real and approved functional changes, and errors in understanding the function originally requested by the users—remember the tire swing cartoon?

EVALUATION OF EXCEPTIONS WILL PROVIDE:

1. Improved change control system
2. Improved perception of functions before requirements finalized
   (Demonstrates which functions are susceptible to misunderstanding)

Transparency 8

Transparency 8. An evaluation of these exceptions will provide information which will help reduce misunderstandings and late changes. This makes control of changes visible and meaningful to both the users and AD/M.

In addition, and just as important, it will help the technical staff improve their perception and understanding of the functions required by the users.

In other words, by demonstrating what kinds of functions and requests are commonly misunderstood at the beginning of a project, we shall learn how to watch out for these "risky" areas and control them properly.

WHAT DO WE MEASURE?

Types of Projects:
- New Development
- Enhancement
- Support

Transparency 9

Transparency 9. To measure effectively the work and activities done by the Application Development and Maintenance staff, it is important that we divide these activities into different functional classifications.

The three major categories we have chosen are new development, enhancement, and support. These will be defined in a few minutes.

WHAT DO WE MEASURE?

Measurement Components
- Work Project
- Work Effort
- Project Attributes

Transparency 10

Transparency 10. For each of these three types of work, there are some key components which must measured.

The work product, which can be thought of as the size or total functionality of the product, is measured similarly in all three cases. We shall talk about some small differences.

Work effort, or the time charged to the activity, has to be defined clearly. And, in all cases, we need to know something about the way the work was done— known here as project attributes.

NEW DEVELOPMENT

Work product
   Function Points Delivered
Work effort
   Analysis, Design, Development, Installation
Project Attributes
   Tools, Techniques, Human Factors, Environment

Transparency 11

Transparency 11. New development projects deliver new applications to the production environment. This may result from either building a system, or from acquiring and installing an application package. In either case, the system is being delivered to meet the business requirements specified by the user.

The work product measure for new development is simply the number of function points delivered. All of the work effort which goes into delivering that product or project, from analysis through installation, is counted. To help in understanding, estimating future project cost, and improving productivity in general, it is important to know what tools and techniques were used, as well as the various human and environmental factors for the project.

ENHANCEMENT

Work product
   Function Points Added, Changed
Work Effort
   Analysis, Design, Development, Installation
Project Attributes
   Tools, Techniques, Human Factors, Environment

Transparency 12

Transparency 12. Enhancement projects deliver modifications to an application which already exists in the production environment. These modifications are always the result of user requests to change or delete existing functions, or to add new functions to the application.

Enhancement, in general, is done in exactly the same steps as new system development. The work product is measured in the same way, as are work effort and project attributes. At a detailed level, of course, some changes are small (a field on a report, for example) and some are very large. These kinds of differences will be accounted for in the work product measure when you receive the more detailed guidelines for Function Point Analysis.

SUPPORT

> *Work product*
> Average Function Points supported during the period
> *Work effort*
> Repair, Prevention, User Support, Conversion
> *Project Attributes*
> Tools, Techniques, Human Factors, Environment

Transparency 13

Transparency 13. Support activities are those which keep the production application up and running. These activities *never* change user functions except to make the system work the way we promised.

Since we are not talking about delivering any new functionality, the work product measure is the average size of the application during a period (a year, for example).

The types of work effort which have to be tracked are the same categories identified and defined by the GUIDE project "Improving Software Maintenance Productivity Through Measurement", namely: Repair (or meeting the warranty), prevention (like increasing disk space or table sizes before system failure), user support (How do I...?, Does the system...?), and conversion to new hardware and software.

WHAT DO WE MEASURE?

> Types of Projects:
> - New Development
> - Enhancement
> - Support

Transparency 9 (repeated)

Transparency 9 (repeated). Even though the measurements of work product, work effort, and project attributes are similar for the three types of projects, they will be measured and evaluated separately. Because of the different skills, tools, and techniques needed and used for these different types of work, comparisons between new development (or enhancement) and support would be meaningless.

CONSIDERATIONS

No 100% perfect measurement program
The important thing:
BEGIN!

Transparency 14

Transparency 14. Planning a measurement program within an organization can be a lengthy process. Presenting theories can lead to many discussions about the practicality or implications of the techniques which have been introduced. If approval to begin the measurement program has to wait until all of the theories can be proven within your own organization, the measurement process will not begin in our lifetimes.

There is no choice. We must begin to collect the data using guidelines based on the experience of other organizations and plan a pilot implementation. Once the data collection gets started, we will have a functioning measurement program. From that point on, modifications will be made in order to have the most effective, realistic, and useful measurements system possible within our organization.

CONSIDERATIONS (continued)

Collecting the data
A *by-product* of project effort
Not a separate recording task

Transparency 15

Transparency 15. If the input data provided to the measurement program requires a lot of preparation by the project staff, the overhead is unwelcome and the quality is questionable. Input data must be produced as a by-product of the natural work of the project. For example, work effort will come from the same time recording system that we use for other purposes. Function Point Analysis data will not initially be considered as a by-product of a project. But after the project staff begins to see the benefits it can provide, the process will be accepted as part of the project deliverables.

CONSIDERATIONS (continued)

Cost of measurement
Data collection and reporting
Less than 1% of project effort

Transparency 16

Transparency 16. Of course, there will be some overhead. Most of that will be because of the person or group interpreting the data, and very little will be involved in the measurement itself. Allan Albrecht recommends one measurement person per 350 AD/M staff, if an independent counting group is used.

During the project, the costs will be very low. Several companies have seen that Function Point Analysis is less than 1/10 of 1% of total project costs. Pay attention, though, because what they mean is that *after* the user requirements are understood, Function Point Analysis is very fast and inexpensive. Of course, this is fair since the cost of understanding the application is part of the cost (and indeed, of the requirements!) of the project and should not be charged to the measurement program.

CONSIDERATIONS (continued)

Quality of the results
GIGO
No benefits with bad data!

Transparency 17

Transparency 17. Speaking of input, remember that the measurement process is just like any other system—garbage in, garbage out.

Of course, management is very concerned about this danger; but before you members of the technical staff say, "So what?", think about the following: If measurement of work effort does not count 10% unpaid overtime on a critical project, then future projects may be estimated based on this bad information and you will be condemned to work 10% unpaid overtime forever! We are exaggerating a little (but just a little!) only to point out that the garbage in is not just garbage out, but rather can have a very negative effect on your future work (and morale).

WHAT DO YOU GET?

- Project cost estimating
- Project control

- Improved tools and techniques
- Morale and working conditions

Transparency 18

Transparency 18. As you are all aware, this presentation is being given to all levels of management and technical staff in our Application Development and Maintenance organization. Let me ask a question: Will a measurement program work if one of the required participants gets lots of work to do and no benefits? Of course not. We are going to make some aggressive claims about the benefits of a measurement program. For each and every one of you, there is something to be gained by ensuring that the measurement program works and works well. Something for everyone!

WHAT DO YOU GET?

Project cost estimating
- *Good* guidelines
- Based on history
- Realistic schedules
- Trackable estimates

Transparency 19

Transparency 19. Now to some specific answers to the question, "What's in it for me?".

Any kind of realistic cost estimating is based both on the gathering of historical information and the understanding of that information. Of course, judgment will still be required—but we are talking about judgment, not guessing, about *10-20%* of the decision-making process, not *100%*. One thing which definitely can be avoided is promising the impossible ("Deliver what you promise, but promise only what you can deliver!"—FitzGerald). Realistic schedules can be met with a lot less pain and "gory" and a lot more fame and glory (or at least, happier users). Naturally, there will always be some assumptions at the beginning of the project which turn out to be wrong. At least we will be able to learn from these for future projects. Often we shall be able to correct them in the middle of the project before the pain starts, or at least before it gets any worse.

WHAT DO YOU GET?

Project control
- Change control

- Scheduling guidelines
- Status feedback

Transparency 20

Transparency 20. One of the key benefits of Function Point Analysis is that it is understood by the users. As a result, it becomes a powerful tool for change control. The major problem in project control is that project scope can change without being noticed soon enough to do something about it—until finally the rate of change (or growth) exceeds the rate of development production. This would be fine if projects always got smaller, but...

With a good cost estimate, schedules and phase ends are easier to define. This applies both to the final delivery and to the intermediate phases. Work effort tracking related to these phases will provide an ongoing status feedback which lets the project manager know if progress is as planned. Better to act early than to panic late!

WHAT DO YOU GET?

Improved tools and techniques
- Realistic choices
- Understood benefits
- Tools match the job

Transparency 21

Transparency 21. Now we really start talking about productivity improvement! We started back at the beginning of this presentation talking about the "promised" improvements in productivity with our new tools and techniques. Do they really help? What is the best tool to choose in a given situation for a given project? We have to make these choices, sometimes project by project, activity by activity, and the best way to make the choice is to understand both the benefits and the potential problems and risks. In other words, the tools have to match the job. If there is a message here, it's this: WE WANT TO WORK SMARTER, NOT HARDER.

WHAT DO YOU GET?

Higher morale
Better working conditions

Transparency 22

Transparency 22. Think through the benefits cited already. They add up to more predictable schedules, less unnecessary work, the feeling (and the reality) that we know where we are and where we are going.

WHAT DO YOU GET?

Senior management

Project management

Technical staff

Transparency 23

Transparency 23. As a summary, it is important to identify the various areas which are supported by the measurement program. These benefits will aid the AD/M staff and management. It will also support any central efforts within the organization to make changes to the environment based on problems and opportunities highlighted by the analysis of the measurement data.

Finally we can answer the question, "Are we improving?".

WHAT DO WE NEED FROM YOU?

Group ownership

Contribute ideas

Commitment

Support

Participation

Transparency 24.

Transparency 24. An effective measurement program is a group effort. Here, at the beginning of the program, we are requesting your ideas and suggestions, as well as your commitment and support.

With the ongoing measurement program, based on the quality of your participation, we shall be able to realize the benefits which are so important to the functioning of the AD/M activities and to your day-to-day work.

To establish an effective measurement program, the co-operation of all concerned is required. Co-operation begins with an understanding of the objectives and scope. Commitment, support, and participation by all will make this program a success. The success of this program will contribute to the success of AD/M, and to the success of our organization.

APPENDIX

Personnel System Case Study Solution and Blank Forms

SOLUTION, PERSONNEL SYSTEM CASE STUDY

SUMMARY SHEET—SIMPLIFIED
APPLICATION: *Personnel*

Business Function	Number	Complexity		Factor		Line Totals	Group Totals
OUTPUTS	23	Simple	*	4	=	92	
	3	Average	*	5	=	15	
	3	Complex	*	7	=	21	
TOTAL:	29						128
INQUIRIES	18	Simple	*	4	=	72	
	6	Average	*	5	=	30	
	0	Complex	*	6	=	0	
	3	Complex	*	7	=	21	
TOTAL:	27						123
INPUTS	74	Simple	*	3	=	222	
	17	Average	*	4	=	68	
	0	Complex	*	6	=	0	
TOTAL:	91						290
FILES	14	Simple	*	7	=	98	
	9	Average	*	10	=	90	
	0	Complex	*	15	=	0	
TOTAL:	23						188
INTERFACES	4	Simple	*	5	=	20	
	4	Average	*	7	=	28	
	0	Complex	*	10	=	0	
TOTAL:	8						48

TOTAL UNADJUSTED FUNCTION POINTS: 777

	Processing Complexity Factors		
Factor	Value	Factor	Value
1. Data communications	5	8. On-line update	5
2. Distributed data/ processing	0	9. Complex processing	2
3. Performance objectives	2	10. Code reusability	0
4. Tight configuration	2	11. Conversion/installation ease	5
5. High transaction rate	0	12. Operational ease	5
6. On-line inquiry/data entry	5	13. Multiple site installation	0
7. End user efficiency	4	14. Facilitate change	5
		TOTAL DEGREE OF INFLUENCE	40

FINAL CALCULATIONS

1. *Adjustment Factor:* $0.65 + (0.01 * 40) = 1.05$

2. *Final Function Point Count:*   777 * 1.05 = 816   Function Points
                                                        Total raw   AF
                                                        FP count

Detail Sheet

Application: Personnel	Function Type: Outputs		
Description:	Simple	Average	Complex
Transaction code file p. 102T	1		
Personnel profiles p. 102M			1
Add/Reactivation Action Report p. 103M		1	
Job Action Report p. 103B	1		
Salary Action Report p. 104M		1	
Org. Assignment Action Report p. 104B	1		
Leave Action Report p. 105T	1		
Employment Type Action Report p. 105M	1		
Query Control Report p. 100M	1		
Merit Pool Report p. 88M	1		
Personnel notification p. 105B	1		
Error notification (data entry & processing) p. 106T	2		
Audit & control notification p. 106M			1
Table Notification Report p. 106B	1		
Security Update Notification Report p. 106T	1		
Ad Hoc Report Template p. 100T		1	
Suspense Data - all individuals p. 83M	1		
Print all 5 tables & directory p. 98M	6		
Print all 4 Security DB files p. 97M	4		
Backup Files —"vital function"			1
*** TOTALS ***	23	3	3

Detail Sheet

Application: Personnel		Function Type: Inquiries	
Description:	Simple	Average	Complex
Menus p. 93T			0/1
Individual current record p. 93B			0/1
Individual history p. 93B			0/1
Individual suspense records p. 94T	1		
Individual records by organization p. 94M		4	
(job, status, organization, payroll ID)			
Table data and directory p. 94M	6		
Audit data p. 94M		1	
Unused payroll ID numbers p. 85M	1		
Security p. 96B		1	
Inquiries before manual corrections p. 95M	9		
Ad Hoc Query Template p. 100T	1		
*** TOTALS ***	18	6	0/3

Detail Sheet

Application: Personnel		Function Type: Inputs	
Description:	Simple	Average	Complex
Sign on/off, including password(s) - standard	1		
Personnel File Master Record add/delete p. 83M	1	1	
Maintain transaction codes p. 84T	3		
Add/reactivate individual p. 84M		2	
Add additional organization assignment p. 85T	1		
Change individual's job p. 86T	1		
Change compensation p. 87T		5	
Provide incentive & special payment p. 88M		1	
Change organization assignment p. 89T		1	
Change personnel status (H/S or S/H) p. 91M		2	
Change personal data p. 91B		1	
Change security data base parameters p. 96M	3		
Security data base transactions p. 96B	12		
Add/change table directory p. 98M	2		
Add/delete/change table entry x 5 p. 98M	15		
Input report specifications p. 98M	21		
Maintain Suspense data base p. 95M	1	2	
Maintain history file p. 93B	1	2	
Correct table data/Personnel data base/			
Suspense data base p. 94B	9		
Maintain unused payroll ID numbers p. 85M	3		
*** TOTALS ***	74	17	0

Detail Sheet

Application: Personnel

Function Type: Files

Description:	Simple	Average	Complex
Personnel Master File p. 94M (indexed 5 ways)		5	
Suspense File p. 83M		1	
Transaction Code File p. 84T	1		
Transaction File p. 83B	1		
Job Table p. 86T	1		
Status Table p. 94M	1		
Organization Assignment Table p. 94M	1		
System User File p. 96B	1		
Views File p. 96B	1		
System Functions File p. 97T	1		
Computer Functions File p. 97T	1		
History File p. 90M		1	
Table directory p. 98M	1		
Unused payroll ID numbers p. 85M	1		
Errors Table p. 83T	1		
Validity/consistency p. 82B		1	
Audit data base p. 106M		1	
Employment Status File p. 91M	1		
Merit Table p. 88M	1		
*** TOTALS ***	14	9	0

Detail Sheet

Application: Personnel

Function Type: Interfaces

Description:	Simple	Average	Complex
Payroll --> Personnel p. 88T	1		
Personnel --> Payroll p. 83B	1		
Change compensation p. 87T		1	
Change compensation and job p. 87T		1	
Change compensation, job, and assignment p. 87T		1	
Change compensation and personnel status p. 87T		1	
Change personal data p. 92M	1		
Security data base p. 96M	1		
*** TOTALS ***	4	4	0

BLANK FORMS

The following nine pages are blank forms you will find useful in managing your own projects. Please make as many copies as needed. GOOD LUCK!

DETAIL SHEET

APPLICATION: _____

DATE: _____

FUNCTION TYPE: _____

SIMPLE   AVERAGE   COMPLEX

DESCRIPTION: _____

*** TOTALS ***   _____

SUMMARY SHEET - SIMPLIFIED

DATE:_____

APPLICATION:_____

Business Function	Number	Complexity		Factor		Line Totals	Group Totals
OUTPUTS		Simple	*	4	=		
		Average	*	5	=		
		Complex	*	7	=		
TOTAL:							
INQUIRIES		Simple	*	4	=		
		Average	*	5	=		
		Complex	*	6	=		
		Complex	*	7	=		
TOTAL:							
INPUTS		Simple	*	3	=		
		Average	*	4	=		
		Complex	*	6	=		
TOTAL:							
FILES		Simple	*	7	=		
		Average	*	10	=		
		Complex	*	15	=		
TOTAL:							
INTERFACES		Simple	*	5	=		
		Average	*	7	=		
		Complex	*	10	=		
TOTAL:							

TOTAL UNADJUSTED FUNCTION POINTS:

DREGER *FUNCTION POINT ANALYSIS* COPYRIGHT 1989 BY PRENTICE-HALL, INC.

Processing Complexity Factors

Factor	Value	Factor	Value
1. Data communications		8. On-line update	
2. Distributed data/ processing		9. Complex processing	
3. Performance objectives		10. Code reusability	
4. Tight configuration		11. Conversion/installation ease	
5. High transaction rate		12. Operational ease	
6. On-line inquiry/data entry		13. Multiple site installation	
7. End user efficiency		14. Facilitate change	
		TOTAL DEGREE OF INFLUENCE	

FINAL CALCULATIONS

1. *Adjustment Factor:*   0.65   +   (0.01   *   _____)   =   _____

2. *Final Function Point Count:*

$$\frac{\text{Total raw}}{\text{FP count}} \quad * \quad \frac{\quad}{\text{AF}} \quad = \quad \underline{\qquad} \text{ Function Points}$$

DREGER *FUNCTION POINT ANALYSIS* COPYRIGHT 1989 BY PRENTICE-HALL, INC.

SUMMARY SHEET - TOTAL MODIFICATION

DATE: _____   APPLICATION: _____

Business Function	SIMPLE			AVERAGE			COMPLEX			Line Totals
	Number	Factor	Total	Number	Factor	Total	Number	Factor	Total	
1. ADDED FUNCTIONS										
OUTPUTS		* 4=			* 5=			* 7=		
INQUIRIES		* 4=			* 5=			* 6=/*7=		
INPUTS		* 3=			* 4=			* 6=		
FILES		* 7=			*10=			*15=		
INTERFACES		* 5=			* 7=			*10=		
TOTAL ADDED								TOTAL	_____	
								ADD	_____	
2. "AFTER" CHANGES										
OUTPUTS		* 4=			* 5=			* 7=		
INQUIRIES		* 4=			* 5=			* 6=/*7=		
INPUTS		* 3=			* 4=			* 6=		
FILES		* 7=			*10=			*15=		
INTERFACES		* 5=			* 7=			*10=		
TOTAL "AFTER"								TOTAL	_____	
CHANGES								CHG$_a$	_____	

DREGER *FUNCTION POINT ANALYSIS* COPYRIGHT 1989 BY PRENTICE-HALL, INC.

SUMMARY SHEET - TOTAL MODIFICATION (continued)

DATE: _____   APPLICATION: _____

Business Function	SIMPLE			AVERAGE			COMPLEX			Line Totals
	Number	Factor	Total	Number	Factor	Total	Number	Factor	Total	
3. DELETED FUNCTIONS										
OUTPUTS		* 4=			* 5=			* 7=		
INQUIRIES		* 4=			* 5=			* 6=/*7=		
INPUTS		* 3=			* 4=			* 6=		
FILES		* 7=			*10=			*15=		
INTERFACES		* 5=			* 7=			*10=		
TOTAL DELETED	_____			_____			TOTAL _____			
							DEL _____			

Processing Complexity Factors

Factor	Before	After	Comments	Factor	Before	After	Comments
1. Data communications				8. On-line update			
2. Distributed data/ processing				9. Complex processing			
3. Performance objectives				10. Code reusability			
4. Tight configuration				11. Conversion/installation ease			
5. High transaction rate				12. Operational ease			
6. On-line inquiry/data entry				13. Multiple site installation			
7. End user efficiency				14. Facilitate change			
				TOTAL DEGREE OF INFLUENCE	DI_b ___	DI_a ___	

FINAL CALCULATIONS

1. *Adjustment Factors:* (AF_b = BEFORE, AF_a = AFTER)

$$AF_b = 0.65 + (0.01 * \frac{\_\_\_}{DI_b}) = \_\_\_ \qquad AF_a = 0.65 + (0.01 * \frac{\_\_\_}{DI_a}) = \_\_\_$$

2. *Final Function Point Count,*

TOTAL *Modification:* $[\underline{\hspace{1cm}} * \underline{\hspace{1cm}}] + [(\underline{\hspace{1cm}} + \underline{\hspace{1cm}}) * \underline{\hspace{1cm}}] = \underline{\hspace{1cm}}$ Function Points

DEL AF_b ADD CHG_a AF_a TOTAL
MODIFICATION

DREGER *FUNCTION POINT ANALYSIS* COPYRIGHT 1989 BY PRENTICE-HALL, INC.

SUMMARY SHEET - NET MODIFICATION

DATE: _____   APPLICATION: _____

Business Function	SIMPLE			AVERAGE			COMPLEX			Line Totals
	Number	Factor	Total	Number	Factor	Total	Number	Factor	Total	
1. ADDED FUNCTIONS										
OUTPUTS		* 4=			* 5=			* 7=		
INQUIRIES		* 4=			* 5=			* 6=/*7=		
INPUTS		* 3=			* 4=			* 6=		
FILES		* 7=			*10=			*15=		
INTERFACES		* 5=			* 7=			*10=		
TOTAL ADDED								TOTAL		
								_____ ADD		_____
2. "AFTER" CHANGES										
OUTPUTS		* 4=			* 5=			* 7=		
INQUIRIES		* 4=			* 5=			* 6=/*7=		
INPUTS		* 3=			* 4=			* 6=		
FILES		* 7=			*10=			*15=		
INTERFACES		* 5=			* 7=			*10=		
TOTAL "AFTER" CHANGES		_____			_____			TOTAL _____ CHGa		_____

DREGER *FUNCTION POINT ANALYSIS* COPYRIGHT 1989 BY PRENTICE-HALL, INC.

SUMMARY SHEET - NET MODIFICATION (continued)

DATE: _____   APPLICATION: _____

Business Function	SIMPLE			AVERAGE			COMPLEX			Line Number Totals
	Number	Factor	Total	Number	Factor	Total	Number	Factor	Total	
3. DELETED FUNCTIONS										
OUTPUTS		* 4=			* 5=			* 7=		
INQUIRIES		* 4=			* 5=			* 6=/*7=		
INPUTS		* 3=			* 4=			* 6=		
FILES		* 7=			*10=			*15=		
INTERFACES		* 5=			* 7=			*10=		
TOTAL DELETED										_____ DEL
4. "BEFORE" FUNCTIONS										
OUTPUTS		* 4=			* 5=			* 7=		
INQUIRIES		* 4=			* 5=			* 6=/*7=		
INPUTS		* 3=			* 4=			* 6=		
FILES		* 7=			*10=			*15=		
INTERFACES		* 5=			* 7=			*10=		
TOTAL "BEFORE" CHANGES										_____ CHG_b

DREGER *FUNCTION POINT ANALYSIS* COPYRIGHT 1989 BY PRENTICE-HALL, INC.

Processing Complexity Factors

Factor	Before	After	Comments	Factor	Before	After	Comments
1. Data communications				8. On-line update			
2. Distributed data/ processing				9. Complex processing			
3. Performance objectives				10. Code reusability			
4. Tight configuration				11. Conversion/installation ease			
5. High transaction rate				12. Operational ease			
6. On-line inquiry/data entry				13. Multiple site installation			
7. End user efficiency				14. Facilitate change			
				TOTAL DEGREE OF INFLUENCE	DI_b _____	_____ DI_a	

FINAL CALCULATIONS

1. *Adjustment Factors:* (AF_b = BEFORE, AF_a = AFTER)

$$AF_b = 0.65 + (0.01 * \underline{\quad DI_b \quad}) = \underline{\quad}$$

$$AF_a = 0.65 + (0.01 * \underline{\quad DI_a \quad}) = \underline{\quad}$$

2. *Final Function Point Count,*   (IMPORTANT: note minus sign!)

NET Modification: $-[(\underline{\quad}_{DEL} + \underline{\quad}_{CHG_b}) * \underline{\quad}_{AF_b}] + [(\underline{\quad}_{ADD} + \underline{\quad}_{CHG_a}) * \underline{\quad}_{AF_a}] = \underline{\quad}$ Function Points

NET MODIFICATION

DREGER *FUNCTION POINT ANALYSIS* COPYRIGHT 1989 BY PRENTICE-HALL, INC.

BIBLIOGRAPHY

"A Programmer Productivity Controversy", *EDP Analyzer*, January 1986.

ACCENT R User's Manual and DEC VAX/VMS 4GL systems generator software, National Information Systems, San Jose, California, 1988.

ALBRECHT, ALLAN J., "AD/M Productivity Measurement and Estimate Validation", IBM, Purchase, New York, 1 November 1984.

ALBRECHT, ALLAN J., "Function Points Help Managers Assess Application, Maintenance Values", *Computerworld Special Report*, pp. 20-21, 26 August 1985.

ALBRECHT, ALLAN J., "Measuring Application Development and Maintenance", unpublished handout from IBM Seminar, 13-16 June 1983.

ALBRECHT, ALLAN J., "Measuring Application Development Productivity", *Proceedings, Joint SHARE/GUIDE/IBM Application Development Symposium*, October 1979, pp. 83-92.

ALBRECHT, ALLAN J. AND JOHN E. GAFFNEY, JR., "Software Function, Source Lines of Code, and Development Effort Prediction: A Software Science Validation", *IEEE Transactions on Software Engineering*, pp. 639-648, November 1983.

BEHRENS, CHARLES A., "Measuring the Productivity of Computer Systems Development Activities with Function Points", *IEEE Transactions on Software Engineering*, pp. 648-652, November 1983.

BOEHM, BARRY W., *Software Engineering Economics*, Prentice-Hall, Englewood Cliffs, New Jersey, 1981.

BROWN, DARLENE, "Function Points User's Manual", Royal Bank of Canada, Toronto, Ontario, 1987.

Counting Practices Manual (draft), International Function Point Users Group, 1987.

DEMARCO, TOM, *Controlling Software Projects*, Yourdon Press, Englewood Cliffs, New Jersey, 1982.

DORR, BRENDA, "Implementing Function Point Analysis in *Your* Organization", contained in *GUIDE International Publication GPP-134*, Chicago, Illinois, 1984.

DREGER, J. BRIAN, lesson plan lecture notes, The Boeing Company, "Project Management for the Boeing Executive" seminar, Wichita, Kansas, 22-26 February 1988.

DREGER, J. BRIAN, lesson plan lecture notes, The Boeing Company, "Structured Systems Analysis and Design", Wichita, Kansas, 1987.

DREGER, J. BRIAN, lesson plan lecture notes, Webster University Graduate School of Business Administration, BUS 608 "Business Information Systems", 1987.

DREGER, J. BRIAN, lesson plan lecture notes, Wichita State University Graduate School of Computer Science, CS 684 "Structured Applications Systems Analysis and Design", 1987.

DREGER, J. BRIAN, *Project Management*, under development.

DRUMMOND, STEVE, "Measuring Applications Development Performance", *Datamation*, pp. 102-108, 15 February 1985.

"Estimating Using Function Points Handbook", GPP-134, GUIDE International Publications, Chicago, Illinois, 1985.

FITZGERALD, JERRY AND ARDRA FITZGERALD, *Fundamentals of Systems Analysis Using Structured Analysis and Design Techniques*, John Wiley & Sons, New York, 1987.

"Function Point Analysis", *LINC Marketing Training Guide*, Unisys Corporation, Detroit, Michigan, 1985.

GUIDE 67 MP1423 project team, "Improving Software Maintenance Productivity Through Measurement", MP1423 Release 4.0, GUIDE 67, Anaheim, California, 1985.

JONES, T. CAPERS, "A Glossary of Software Management, Measurement, and Estimation", Software Productivity Research, Inc., Cambridge, Massachusetts, 1988.

JONES, T. CAPERS, "A Short History of Function Points and Feature Points", Software Productivity Research, Inc., Cambridge, Massachusetts, 1988.

JONES, T. CAPERS, "Function-Point Metrics: Key to Improved Productivity", *Information Week*, pp. 26-27, 23 February 1987.

JONES, T. CAPERS, "How Not to Measure Programming Productivity", *Computerworld*, p. 65, 13 January 1986.

JONES, T. CAPERS, Interview in *Computerworld Special Report*, 28 May 1984.

JONES, T. CAPERS, *Measuring Software*, under development.

JONES, T. CAPERS, "Productivity Gauge Changing", *Computerworld*, pp. 33-37, 19 November 1984.

JONES, T. CAPERS, *Programming Productivity*, McGraw-Hill, New York, 1986.

JONES, T. CAPERS, *Programming Productivity: Issues of the Eighties, IEEE Catalogue #* EHO 186-7, 1982.

JONES, T. CAPERS, *SPQR/20 User Guide*, Software Productivity Research, Inc., Cambridge, Massachusetts, 1987.

JONES, T. CAPERS, "The Limits of Programming Productivity", *Proceedings, Joint SHARE/ GUIDE/IBM Application Development Symposium*, October 1979, pp. 77-82.

KUNKLER, J. E., *A Co-operative Industry Study Software Development Productivity*, Xerox Corporation, May 1983.

LUDLUM, DAVID A., "Measuring DP Efficiency, Quality", *Computerworld*, pp. 71-74, 11 August 1986.

MARTIN, JAMES, *Fourth-Generation Languages, Volume I*, Chapter 4, Prentice-Hall, Englewood Cliffs, New Jersey, 1985.

NOTH, THOMAS, *Aufwandschatzung von DV - Projekten*, Springer-Verlag, the Netherlands (translator unknown), 1984.

RUDOLPH, EBERHARD E., *Function Point Analysis Cookbook*, Burroughs (Unisys) Working Paper, Detroit, Michigan, March 1983.

RUDOLPH, EBERHARD E., "Productivity in Computer Application Development", Burroughs (Unisys) Document 1172335, Detroit, Michigan, 1984.

RUDOLPH, EBERHARD E., "Productivity in Computer Application Development", Department of Management Studies, Working Paper #9, University of Auckland, March 1983.

RUDOLPH, EBERHARD E., "Software Development Productivity - How to Measure It", *NZ Interface*, pp. 46-49, April 1983.

RUDOLPH, EBERHARD E. AND GIL SIMPSON, *Evaluation of a Fourth Generation Language*, Burroughs (Unisys) Internal Working Paper, 1983.

SCHIMANSKI, M. KAY, lesson plan lecture notes, Unisys Corporation Customer Education Course EP 6379, "Function Point Analysis", Lisle, Illinois, 10-12 February 1986.

"To Improve Productivity, Quantitatively Measure DP Quality", *Data Management*, pp. 34-36, April 1987.

Unisys Corporation Customer Education Course EP 6379, "Function Point Analysis" Student Guide, 1985.

VACCA, JOHN, "Function Points: The New Measure of Software", *Computerworld*, pp. 99-108, 18 November 1985.

VERNER, JUNE M. AND GRAHAM TATE, "A Model for Software Sizing", *Journal of Systems & Software*, pp. 173-177, June 1987.

Index

A

Abbreviations, used in other FPA works, 9

ACCENT R (National Information Systems 4GL), 133, 134, 135, 137, 139

Access Technology, Inc., 137

Accuracy, Function Point Analysis, 4, 5, 77, 78, 79, 119, 132–33, 138–39, 144–45

Accuracy, of predictors, 79

ADD, 111, 117, 118

Added business functions, 108–9, 109–112, 117–18

Additional factors, why not used, 15, 20, 24, 31, 38

Adjusted function point total, 8, 62, 71, 76–77

Adjustment factor, 62, 63, 66, 71, 77, 110, 111, 112, 117, 118, 125, 126, 128, 130, 131

AF_a, 111, 117, 118

AF_b, 110, 117, 118

Albrecht, Allan J., 4, 108, 144

Applicability of FPA to multiple languages, 4, 136

Application boundary, 8, 9

Application performance objectives, 63, 64, 68

Applications backlog, 144

Approved functions, 6, 9, 11, 14, 20, 24, 30, 32, 38, 63, 66, 79, 108, 115

B

Backlog, applications, 144

Backup file, 6–7, 11, 12, 30, 79

"Ball park" estimate, 32

Batch AF, typical minimum value, 71

Bibliography, 174–76

Blank forms, 165–73

Brown, Darlene, 144

Bug, 108, 137

Burroughs Corporation, 133